Jo

CW00689923

A Summary

All booklets are published thanks to the generous support of the members of the Catholic Truth Society

CATHOLIC TRUTH SOCIETY
PUBLISHERS TO THE HOLY SEE

CONTENTS

——————— PREFACE ———————

The Pontificate of John Paul II has been extraordinary in
every way. The first non-Italian pope in over 450 years
has been seen in person by more people than any other
human being in history. He has visited 125 countries. He
has canonized over 470 new saints and beatified more
than 1200 witnesses to the Faith. He has been shot,
ridiculed by many in the secular world and yet voted
Time Life 'man of the year' in 1994. It is however, the
wealth of teaching on a scale which the Church has
never seen before, which is surveyed in this book. Karol
Wojtyla has applied his unique mind and personal and
pastoral experience to a host of issues.

Some 13 Encyclicals, 11 Apostolic Exhortations and
34 Apostolic letters as well as countless other documents,
homilies, audiences and speeches have meant that very
few subjects have been left untouched by his pontificate.
Yet it is clear that going back even to his formative years
in the underground seminary during World War II some
subjects have been especially close to his heart and his
considerable mind. Since his election in 1978 these have
been explored systematically using all the instruments
available to the See of Peter as well as some new ones
(for example, the Maundy Thursday *Letter to Priests*).

As one of the architects of the major documents of
Vatican II, the Council teachings are echoed strongly in
everything the Pope has taught. Its redefinition of the

role of all the baptised has prompted John Paul's teaching on and challenge to the whole church, laity and clergy alike. His experience of Nazism and Communism have given an impetus to Catholic Social Teaching that has truly brought it to its maturity. His time as Professor of Social Ethics in Lublin and immense pastoral experience among families and students, has uniquely qualified him to reiterate and express in new and extraordinary terms the Church's teaching on women, sexual ethics and the theology of the body. His training as a philosopher has spurred him to search for a 'dialogue with culture', the fruit of which has seen a remarkable discourse of the Church with science and philosophy. His roots in Poland which stands between East and West have impelled him to look for ecumenical and interreligious bridges never imagined before. All of which has been undertaken with a firm Trinitarian outlook, in true devotion to Mary and with the missionary zeal to respond to Christ's call to "go therefore, [and] make disciples of all the Nations" *(Mt 28:19)*.

The thrust and direction of the Pope's writings and speeches on these major themes are summarised in this booklet. Each chapter is written by an expert in the field, clearly identifying and defining the new contribution of the pope's teaching. It is hoped that this booklet will be a useful companion to the great journey that the Church has made in the last 23 years, led by the pastor who will surely be called John Paul the Great.

About the Authors

Thomas G. Weinandy is a Capuchin priest and the Warden of Greyfriars, Oxford. He is Lecturer and Tutor in History and Doctrine at the University of Oxford. He has written many articles and a number of books which include: *Sacrament of Mercy: A Spiritual and Practical Guide to Confession*; *The Father's Spirit of Sonship: Reconceiving the Trinity*; and *Does God Suffer?*

Charles Whitehead has served for 10 years as the President of ICCRS, International Catholic Charismatic Renewal Services. He is now responsible for ICCOWE, the International Charismatic Consultation on World Evangelisation, and is active in a number of organisations at parish, diocesan, and national level. He is also an author and international conference speaker and lives with his wife in Gerrards Cross, England.

Fr. Philip Egan is a priest of the Diocese of Shrewsbury. He is currently a Lecturer in Foundational Theology and the Director of Studies at St. Mary's College, Oscott, the major seminary in the Archdiocese of Birmingham, England.

Rodger Charles is Lecturer and Tutor in Moral and Pastoral Theology at Campion Hall, Oxford and has been researching, writing and lecturing on Catholic social teaching for over thirty years. His main publications on the subject are *The Social Teaching of Vatican II* (1982), the two volume *Christian Social Witness and Teaching: the Catholic Tradition from Genesis to Centesimus Annus* (1998) and the short *Introduction to Catholic Social Teaching* (1999).

Michele M. Schumacher is an external scientific collaborator in the theology department (dogmatic chair) at the University of Fribourg, Switzerland. Her doctorate from the John Paul II Institute in Washington D.C. is on the theology of mediation in the work of Hans Urs von Balthasar. She has written on the theologies of women, marriage, and redemption, and on what John Paul II calls a "new feminism". She lives in Switzerland with her husband and their two small children.

Christopher West is an international lecturer on John Paul II's *Theology of the Body* and author of two books on the subject: *Good News About Sex & Marriage* and *The Theology of the Body Explained.* He is also a visiting professor of the "Theology of the Body" at the John Paul II Institute in Melbourne, Australia. He lives outside Denver in the United States with his wife and two sons.

David Carter is an associate lecturer and research associate in Religious Studies with the Open University. He is a Methodist Local Preacher and member of the British Roman Catholic-Methodist Committee for dialogue. He is married with one daughter and lives in Surrey, England.

Bishop Michael Fitzgerald is currently the Secretary of the Pontifical Council for Interreligious Dialogue. A member of the Society of Missionaries of Africa, he was Director of the Pontifical Institute of Arabic and Islamic Studies, Rome. His writings include, *Catalysts* (with R. Dionne) and *Signs of Dialogue: Christian Encounter with Muslims* (with R. Caspar) as well as numerous articles on interreligious dialogue in general and Christian-Muslim relations in particular.

Neville Kyrke-Smith studied theology at Worcester College, Oxford. He was in the Anglican ministry for 8 years and his marriage to Jean - a Graduate in Russian - sparked an interest in Eastern Europe. After following her into the Catholic Church in 1990, he became National Director of Aid to the Church in Need. He travels widely promoting its charitable work including to Ukraine, Belarus, Russia and Siberia.

John Saward is Senior Professor at the International Theological Institute in Gaming, Austria. He is the author of six books, including: *Christ is the Answer: The Christ-Centred Teaching of Pope John Paul II.* He is also a visiting professor at the Newman Institute in Ballina, Ireland, and at the John Paul II Institute in Melbourne, Australia.

Anthony Bosnick is Director of Publications and Editor of *Share The Word Magazine* for the Paulist National Catholic Evangelization Association, Washington D.C., USA. His professional and volunteer work for over 25 years has centered on Catholic education, communications, publications, and social outreach. He lives in the Washington D.C. area with his wife and four children.

Note on abbreviations

References to Papal and other documents in the text are frequently made in abbreviated form. A full list of abbreviations is provided on page 176.

JOHN PAUL II AND HIS TEACHING ON THE TRINITY

By THOMAS G. WEINANDY, OFM, CAP.

On 16 October 1978, Cardinal Karol Wojtyla, Archbishop of Krakow, became Pope John Paul II. His first public utterance, proclaimed to the cheering crowd in St. Peter's Square, was: 'Praised be Jesus Christ!' John Paul has made that proclamation throughout his entire pontificate, and he has done so throughout the entire world. While this proclamation centres on Jesus Christ, since he is the one who is to be praised and acknowledged as Lord and Saviour, yet this proclamation is trinitarian. St. Paul assures us that 'no one can say "Jesus is Lord" except by the Holy Spirit' *(1 Corinthians 12:3)*. Moreover, this Spirit inspired proclamation of Jesus' Lordship is 'to the glory of God the Father' *(Phil. 2:11)*. It is not surprising then that among the first of John Paul's encyclicals, which commenced his pontificate and so established its focus and theme, should be on the persons of the Trinity. His first encyclical on Jesus, *Redemptor Hominis (The Redeemer of Man)*, appeared in 1979, his second on God the Father, *Dives in Misericordia* (*Rich in Mercy*), in 1980, and on the Holy Spirit, *Dominum et Vivificantem* (*The Lord and Giver of Life*), in 1986. These three encyclicals prophetically anticipated the final three years of preparation for the celebration of the Millennium Jubilee in the year 2000. 1997 was dedicated to the Holy Spirit, 1998 to Jesus Christ, 1999 to the Father, and the year 2000 to the Trinity itself. Let us examine some of the main topics within these trinitarian encyclicals.

Redemptor Hominis - on Jesus Christ

John Paul opens his first encyclical with the words:

'The Redeemer of man, Jesus Christ, is the centre of the universe and of history. To him go my thoughts and my heart in this solemn moment of the world that the Church and the whole family of present-day humanity are now living' *(RH 1)*.

That Jesus Christ, as the incarnate Son God who died for the sin of humankind and rose as the Lord of all history imparting the new life of the Holy Spirit, is at the very heart of the Pope's pontificate, for he believes that Jesus is at the very centre of all human life and of all history. If John Paul is to fulfil the ministry of St. Peter in this momentous age, he believes that he must feed the lambs *of* Christ. To do so he must feed them *on* Christ himself *(see RH 7)*.

Our spirit is set in one direction, the only direction for our intellect, will and heart is - towards Christ our Redeemer, towards Christ, the Redeemer of man. We wish to look towards him - because there is salvation in no one else but him, the Son of God - repeating what Peter said: 'Lord, to whom shall we go? You have the words of eternal life' *(RH 7)*.

For John Paul this message of Jesus as Redeemer is of the utmost importance. He perceives a world of unimaginable suffering due to hatred, violence, poverty, greed, injustice and war *(see RH 13-17)*. In the midst of this untold human suffering, ultimately due to sin, only Jesus, the Redeemer, can free humankind from sin and so the suffering that it encounters. Jesus, as Redeemer, is recreating the world and specifically recreating humankind. Echoing the teaching of the Second Vatican Council that the mystery of the Incarnation brings light upon the mystery of man, the Pope states:

'Christ is the new Adam, in the very revelation of the mystery of the Father and of his love, *fully reveals man to himself* and brings to light his most high calling'. ... Human nature, by the very fact that it was assumed, not absorbed, in him, has been raised in us also to a dignity beyond compare. For, by the Incarnation, he, the Son of God, *in a certain way united himself with each man (RH 8, see 14)*.

This is an absolutely crucial teaching within John Paul's thought. Firstly, as the incarnate Son, Jesus is the New Adam, who through his work of redemption brings about a new creation in the Spirit.

Secondly, as the New Adam, Jesus reveals to man what man, recreated in the Spirit, is called to be. Like Jesus man is to live a sinless life of virtue, a life of truth and love, fulfiling all the human potential that each man and woman possesses. This human fulfilment is realized within all authentic human vocations and endeavours, whether that vocation to be to the priesthood, religious life, marriage or the single state, or that endeavour be intellectual, scientific, artistic, literary, political or technological. Moreover, man, in imitation of the Son, is to be obedient sons and daughters of the Father. Ultimately, as Jesus lived by the Holy Spirit, so too must those who are also children of the Father. This is the supreme dignity bestowed on humankind by the Father through Christ in the Holy Spirit.

Thirdly, John Paul significantly insists that as all human beings are joined to the first Adam and so to Adam's sin, so now all human beings are now joined to the New Adam and so, in some manner, to the 'newness' of the New Adam. Human life is no longer the same for the Son of God, in becoming incarnate, has inextricably woven himself within the whole of human history and so firmly joined himself to all men.

For the Pope, Jesus' work of redemption testifies specifically to the work of divine mercy. 'This revelation of love is also described as mercy; and in man's history this revelation of love and mercy has taken a form and a name: that of Jesus Christ' *(RH 9)*.

The Church unceasingly contemplates this mystery of Christ for 'the Church knows with all certainty of faith that the Redemption that took place through the Cross has definitively restored his dignity to man and given back meaning to his life in the world, a meaning that was lost to a considerable extent because of sin' *(RH 10)*. For the Pope, while sin and death appear to have dominion over humankind, Jesus, the Redeemer, through his cross has vanquished sin and by his resurrection has restored to humankind eternal and incorruptible life. The fundamental task of the Church then for John Paul is to foster a union of faith and grace between each human person and Christ.

The Church wishes to serve this single end: that each person may be able to find Christ, in order that Christ may walk with each person the path of life, with the power of the truth about man and the world that is contained in the mystery of the Incarnation and the Redemption and with the power of the love that is radiated by that truth *(RH 13)*.

In order for the Church to fulfil its divinely appointed mission of co-operating in Christ's work of redemption, it too must be united to each human person. John Paul teaches, therefore, that it is through the Church's union with Christ that it becomes united to each human being.

The Church has only one life: that which is given her by her Spouse and Lord. Indeed, precisely because Christ united himself with her in his mystery of Redemption, the Church must be strongly united with each man *(RH 18)*.

The Church thus is responsible for divine truth and so shares in the prophetic ministry of Christ himself. This means that the Church not only seeks to better understand this truth for itself but also that it might be better equipped to proclaim it to others 'in all its saving power, its splendour and its profundity joined with simplicity' *(RH 19)*.

Integral to this saving mission of Christ and his Church are the sacraments. The Church in leading men and women to Christ first leads them, through repentance and faith, to the waters of Baptism for there they die with Christ so as to be reborn in the new life of the Holy Spirit. In this sacrament men and women are first united to Christ, but this union finds its most perfect expression in the Eucharist. 'For by Christ's will there is in this Sacrament a continual renewing of the mystery of the Sacrifice of himself that Christ offered to the Father on the altar of the Cross, a Sacrifice that the Father accepted' *(RH 20)*. Moreover, it is within the

Eucharist that Christians encounter their fullest communion with the risen Christ on earth for he is truly
present under the forms of bread and wine. Thus, it is
through the Eucharist that Christ's presence in our
midst is most fully perceived. John Paul, therefore,
declares that the Eucharist is 'at one and the same time
a Sacrifice-Sacrament, a Communion-Sacrament, and
a Presence-Sacrament' *(RH 20)*. The Eucharist is truly
then, in keeping with Christ the Redeemer of mankind,
the sacrament of our salvation.

Dives in Misericordia - on God the Father

Jesus, the Redeemer of man, was sent by the Father of
mercies and so reveals that the Father is the 'God, who
is rich in mercy' *(Ephesians 2:4)*. This is the theme of
John Paul's second encyclical, *Dives in Misericoridia*.
To see Jesus is to behold the 'Father of mercies and God
of all comfort' *(2 Corinthians 1:3)*. So much did the
Father have mercy upon us that, even though we were
sinners, he 'sent the Son into the world, not to condemn
the world, but that the world might be saved through
him' *(John 3:17)*. This is expressly witnessed in the
cross. 'God shows his love for us in that while we were
yet sinners Christ died for us' *(Romans 5:8)*. Thus, for
the Pope, Jesus incarnates the mercy of the Father.

Not only does he [Jesus] speak of it [mercy] and
explain it by the use of comparisons and parables, but

above all *he himself makes incarnate* and personifies it. *He himself, in a certain sense, is mercy.* To the person who sees it in him - one finds it in him - God becomes 'visible' in a particular way as the Father 'who is rich in mercy' *(DM 2)*.

In the Old Testament God begins to manifest his mercy in that he made a covenant with his chosen people and forgave their sins when they were disloyal to that covenant *(see DM 4)*. Moses declared that he is a 'God merciful and gracious, slow to anger, and abounding in steadfast love and faithfulness' *(Exodus 34:6)*. However, it is again Jesus and specifically his death on the cross that reveals the depth of the Father's mercy. Human sin demanded, in justice, that reparation be made to God, a reparation that went beyond what was humanly possible. It is the Father of mercy who provides a saviour in the person of his Son to make such a sacrifice of love.

In this way *the Cross of Christ*, on which the Son, consubstantial with the Father, *renders full justice to God*, is also *a radical revelation of mercy*, or rather of the love that goes against what constitutes the very root of evil in the history of man: against sin and death *(DM 8)*.

At the end of time, in the eschatological fulfilment, mercy will be revealed as love. However, 'while in the temporal phase, in human history, which is at the same time the history of sin and death, love must be revealed above all as mercy and must also be actualized as mercy' *(DM 8)*. Thus the resurrection, for John Paul, equally reveals the mercy of the Father. Not only did the Father manifest his mercy in raising his Son gloriously from the dead, but also, in so doing, promised, in his mercy, to raise up all who believe in his Son. The resurrection at the end of time is the everlasting witness to the mercy of the Father!

In Jesus' death and resurrection the Father is acting out in real life the parable of the Prodigal Son. The younger son did not merely squander his inheritance, but more so squandered his sonship. This is his true loss. In contrast to the faithless son, 'the father of the prodigal son *is faithful to his fatherhood, faithful to the love* that he had always lavished on his son' *(DM 6)*. The fidelity of the father 'is totally concentrated upon the humanity of the lost son, upon his dignity' *(DM 6)*. As the Pope notes, the father does not humiliate his returning son, but, in his mercy and love, restores his lost dignity. He raises him up to the status of once more being a son *(see DM 6)*. Thus, the true meaning of mercy is not just looking in compassion at moral, physical or material evil. 'Mercy is manifested in its true and proper aspect when it restores to value, promotes and *draws good from all the forms of evil* existing in the world and in man'

(DM 6). The Father of mercy restores this dignity to human beings through the salvific work of his incarnate Son who pours out his Spirit upon all who believe recreating them into sons and daughters of the Father.

It is this divine mercy, the Pope believes, that is desperately needed within our world. Only if human beings know the mercy of the Father will they in turn show mercy to one another - a mercy that overcomes hatred, prejudice, injustice, poverty, and war *(see DM 10)*. Mercy must enliven justice and mercy must be expressed, above all, in forgiveness *(see DM 14)*. This is the mission of the Church.

The Church must bear witness to the mercy of God revealed in Christ, in the whole of his mission as Messiah, *professing it* in the first place as a salvific truth of faith and as necessary for a life in harmony with faith, and then *seeking to introduce it and to make it incarnate in the lives* both of her faithful and as far as possible in the lives of all people of good will *(DM 12)*.

Thus the Church must attempt to bring this mercy to bear upon all levels of society and within every concrete situation, but most of all through conversion. 'Conversion to God always consists *in discovering his mercy*' *(DM 13)*.

John Paul concludes his encyclical by himself imploring God for his mercy. 'It likewise obliges me to have recourse to that mercy and to beg for it at this difficult, critical phase of the history of the Church and of the world, as we approach the end of the second millennium' *(DM 15)*.

Dominum et Vivificantem - on the Holy Spirit

John Paul's trinitarian encyclicals culminate with his third on the Holy Spirit. He states that all three encyclicals find their inspiration in Paul's proclamation: 'The grace of the Lord Jesus Christ and the love of God and the fellowship of the Holy Spirit be with you' *(2 Corinthians 13:14)*. The love of the Father is seen in his mercifully sending his Son into the world so that through him humankind may obtain the grace of salvation. That grace of salvation is principally the gift of the Holy Spirit through whom humankind attains fellowship with the Father and the Son.

In the first part of his encyclical John Paul, founding his thought on the Gospel of John *(DV chapters 13-17)*, professes that the Holy Spirit is the Spirit of the Father and the Son. Together they have sent their Spirit into the world to continue the work of salvation willed by the Father and accomplished through his incarnate Son. At the Last Supper Jesus promised that, even though he would be leaving them, the Father would nonetheless send them another Paraclete, that is another counselor, intercessor, or advocate *(see John*

14:16-17). One of the primary duties of the Holy Spirit would be to 'teach you all things, and bring to your remembrance all that I have said to you' *(John 14:26).* Thus, the Holy Spirit is the Spirit of truth who reveals and validates the Word of Father - Jesus' Gospel. The Holy Spirit 'will help people to understand the correct meaning of the content of Christ's message.... He will ensure that in the Church there will always continue *the same truth* which the apostles heard from their Master' *(DV 4).* Because of the Spirit of truth the Church will never fall into error, for the Holy Spirit 'inspires, guarantees and convalidates the faithful transmission of this revelation in the preaching and writing of the Apostles' *(DV 5).* Equally, the Holy Spirit is at the heart of faith. Faith is 'the work of the Spirit of truth and the result of his action in man. Here the Holy Spirit is to be man's supreme guide and the light of the human spirit' *(DV 6).*

While the Father intended from the beginning that humankind should share in the intimate life of the Trinity through the Holy Spirit, sin has disrupted that fellowship. However, Jesus has come to free humankind from this sin, and the Spirit was present in this great event. 'The conception and birth of Jesus Christ are in fact the greatest work accomplished by the Holy Spirit in the history of creation and salvation: the supreme grace' *(DV 50).* Not only does the

Spirit bring about the Incarnation, but also 'with the mystery of the Incarnation there opens in a new way the source of this divine life in the history of mankind: the Holy Spirit' *(DV 52)*. Moreover, through the Cross Jesus, acting in the Spirit, once more made fellowship with God possible.

The Son of God, Jesus Christ, as man, in the ardent prayer of his Passion, enabled the Holy Spirit, who had already penetrated the inmost depths of his humanity, to transform that humanity into a perfect sacrifice through the act of his death as the victim of love on the Cross *(DV 40)*.

The Holy Spirit is the primary fruit of the Cross. The Cross marks 'the new beginning of God's self-communication to man in the Holy Spirit' *(DV 14)*. From the Cross Jesus breathed forth the new life of his Spirit and from his side flowed the cleansing water of his Spirit *(see John 19:34)*. This Spirit, now dwelling within those who believe, brings a 'supernatural vitality'. For the Pope, through sanctifying grace, there now exists an intimate relationship 'between the uncreated Spirit and the created human spirit' *(DV 52)*.

Sin, then, is a 'contradiction to the presence of the Spirit of God' for sin renders human beings unholy *(DV 13)*. The Holy Spirit convicts the world of sin so as to make it holy *(see John 16:8)*. The Pope summarizes the twofold work of the Holy Spirit.

Conversion requires convincing of sin; it includes the interior judgement of the conscience, and this, being a proof of the action of the Spirit of truth in man's inmost being, becomes at the same time a new beginning of the bestowal of grace and love: 'Receive the Holy Spirit'. Thus in this 'convincing concerning sin' we discover a double gift: the gift of the truth of conscience and the gift of the certainty of redemption *(DV 31)*.

John Paul emphasizes that the Holy Spirit is the personal love shared by the Father and the Son. 'He is Person-Love. He is Person-Gift' *(DV 10)*. It is this Spirit-Gift as Spirit-Love that binds Christians to the Father and the Son, and in so doing transforms them into the likeness of Jesus, the Son, so making them children of the Father, enabling them to cry out, in unison with Jesus, 'Abba, Father' *(see Romans 8:15-16)*. Thus, following the lead of the Second Vatican Council, John Paul sees the Holy Spirit as the 'soul of the church' for it is the Spirit who is the principle of life, strength, vitality and union of all God's people *(DV 26)*. Moreover, it is the Spirit who enlivens and compels the Church to fulfil its divinely inspired mission.

With the coming of the Spirit they (the Apostles) felt capable of fulfiling the mission entrusted to them. They felt full of strength. It is precisely this that the Holy Spirit worked in them, and this is continually at work in the Church, through their successors *(DV 25)*.

The Holy Spirit compels the Church to preach the Lordship of Jesus to the glory of God the Father. In so doing the Holy Spirit is equally engendering within the Church a longing for Jesus to return in glory for this is the goal of the Spirit's work - by the Holy Spirit, on that last day, every knee will bow and every tongue proclaim that Jesus is indeed Lord, and so finally receive the glory and honour he alone deserves. For John Paul, the ardent prayer of the Church, prayed continually in the Spirit as the bride of Christ, is: Come, Lord Jesus! *(see DV 65-66)*.

Conclusion

Pope John Paul, through his trinitarian encyclicals, has clearly taught that each person of the Trinity is intimately involved in the salvation of the world. It is the Father who sent forth his Son and it is the incarnate Jesus, who through his passion and death, has won for us the gift of the Holy Spirit. This Spirit, in turn, unites the believer to Jesus and so to his work of salvation, and in so doing transforms the believer into a child of the Father. Thus Christians participate in the intimate divine life of the Trinity itself - this is the divine purpose and goal of human life itself.

THE VOCATION AND MISSION OF THE LAY FAITHFUL

BY CHARLES WHITEHEAD

To help us appreciate the importance of Pope John Paul II's teaching on the role of the laity in *Christifideles Laici,* and to better understand why he gives his support to the new lay movements and ecclesial communities, we need to look both forwards and backwards. We will find our context for his teaching as we look at the needs of the future Church and at the attitudes of the historical Church.

The Challenges of the Future

How will the Church adapt if in ten to fifteen years time we have in many countries, including England and Wales, only about half the number of priests we have today? What will this mean for the Church? It's a very important question and one that we cannot afford to ignore. One thing is immediately obvious - lay people will have to be more and more involved, not only in bringing the Gospel to the secular society in which we are now living, but also in taking on spiritual areas of ministry and service in building up the Church. This will involve us in catechetics, liturgy, spiritual formation and direction, pastoral care, evangelisation, chaplaincy work in schools, universities, prisons, and hospitals, in addition to all the administration and social work already done in our parishes and dioceses. Are we ready for these new challenges? If this is what the future holds we need to be taking action now to prepare lay men and women for the roles they will have to play. Pope John Paul II seems to be well aware of this, and is beginning to prepare the Church for what lies ahead. So the role of the laity was the subject discussed at the 1987 Synod of Bishops, resulting in *Christifideles Laici*, the first comprehensive Apostolic Exhortation on the calling and mission of lay people in the Church.

The Heritage of the Past

Before the Second Vatican Council, there was little understanding of the place of lay people in the Church and in the world. Why was this? In the New Testament there had been no structural distinction between clergy and laity. Of course there were different ministries, but no separating structure. This gave way to a period when the Church adopted the Roman system of rankings, and so clear distinctions between the roles of clergy and laity became established. The problem which then arose was that distinctions became differences, and separation soon became subordination, and the contribution of the laity to the mission of the Church became less and less important. In 1850 a bishop told Cardinal Newman "The province of the laity is to shoot, to hunt, and to entertain". In similar vein, it has often been joked that the laity are there to pay, pray, and obey. With attitudes like these it's no wonder that Pope Boniface VIII was able to state: "Antiquity shows us that the laity has always been hostile to the clergy". Pope Pius X confirmed clerical fears of the laity when he described modernism as "A most pernicious doctrine which would make of the laity a factor of progress in the Church". But there were signs of change when Pope Pius XII stated:

"Lay believers are in the front line of Church life; for them the Church is the animating principle of human society. Therefore, they in particular ought to have an ever-clearer consciousness not only of belonging to the Church, but of being the Church, that is to say, the community of the faithful on earth under the leadership of the Pope, the common Head, and of the bishops in communion with him. They are the Church" *(Discourse, February 20 1946)*.

In the 1950s, Yves Congar started writing about the importance of a theology of the laity, pointing out that

they were fully members of the Church and not second class citizens or an under-class of the clergy. This
was progress, but how did we get from here to a position where lay people may well be running parishes in
the Church of the future?

Second Class Citizens?

In the preparations for the Second Vatican Council, it
became clear that one of the keys to our view of the
Church is a proper understanding of the respective
roles of the clergy and the laity. *Lumen Gentium*
began to explain the distinctions, and in section 31
defined the laity as "all the faithful except those in
Holy Orders and those who belong to a religious state
approved by the Church". This is still a limited
expression of what it means to be a lay person in the
Church - we know we are not clergy, nor are we in
approved religious orders - so many people were still
asking: "Who are the laity - are they really second
class citizens?"

It is not Permissible for Anyone to Remain Idle

The answer begins to emerge in the 1987 Synod on
the Laity, which developed the theological position
we have before us today. *Christifideles Laici*, to
give the document its Latin title, is therefore the
presentation of the role and mission of the lay mem-

bers of Christ's faithful people. In section 3 Pope John Paul II tells us:

"The basic meaning of this Synod and the most precious fruit desired as a result of it, is the lay faithful's hearkening to the call of Christ the Lord to work in his vineyard, to take an active, conscientious and responsible part in the mission of the Church in this great moment in history, made especially dramatic by occurring on the threshold of the Third Millennium. A new state of affairs today both in the Church and in social, economic, political and cultural life, calls with a particular urgency for the action of the lay faithful. If lack of commitment is always unacceptable, the present time renders it even more so. It is not permissible for anyone to remain idle".

A brief over-view of the Synod's work will give us a much better understanding of the mission to which we are all called through our common baptism. The Exhortation is divided into five chapters preceded by an Introduction and ending with an Appeal and a Prayer. To carry the teaching, Pope John Paul II uses two related Scripture passages, the vine and the branches *(John 15)* and the labourers in the vineyard *(Matthew 20)*. The central image is Jesus Christ, the true vine and the source of our spiritual life, and we his disciples as the branches. The other image is that of the vineyard, representing the world which needs to be transformed by the Gospel message. The call to work in the vineyard is addressed to all of us, and there is an urgency about this call. This is not the time or place for idleness. Christifideles Laici is an exhortation - an appeal, an invitation, an urgent request - it's a call to mobilisation. As such it is addressed to the whole Church, but particularly to the laity.

Jesus Christ, the Hope of Humanity

In the Introduction we are presented with the parable of the vineyard from Matthew's Gospel chapter 20, highlighting the Lord's invitation "You go into my vineyard too". We are reminded that this invitation is addressed to everyone - we are *all* called to labour in the Lord's vineyard. With the pressing needs of the world today, the Lord should never have to ask us "Why do you stand here idle all day?" In the past we may have taken on a passive role, but this is no longer acceptable. Culture and society are now controlled by secular forces, which means religion has little influence. With this march of secularism, the growth of religious indifference and atheism, the violation of human dignity, and the increase in conflict in the world, now is the time to present Jesus Christ, the hope of humanity. This is the task of the lay faithful, because we are more involved in this culture than the clergy are. So we have a duty and a responsibility to make the Gospel present in our family life, our places of work, in politics, the arts, sport, the media, and in the whole of society. We, the laity, are the Church present in the world.

The first chapter then reminds us that baptism is the source of every Christian's dignity and identity, and it is through baptism that we are called to a life of holiness and service, inspired by the Holy Spirit. Chapter two looks at our place in the Church, and our participation in her life and mission through our gifts (charisms) and ministry. The third chapter deals with the shared responsibility of every lay Christian for the mission of the Church, and emphasises the need for a new evangelisation of individuals and society as a whole. We are encouraged to live, to speak, and to make present the Gospel wherever we are. Chapter four looks at the wide variety of callings in the Church and in society, with particular emphasis on the status and role of women. We are all called to work together to build the Kingdom. In the final chapter we are exhorted to be fruitful, with an emphasis on the importance of our own particular calling, so that we may grow into mature Christian men and women. We are reminded that our on-going life-long formation is not just the privilege of a few, but the right of all. In this document we find at last a positive and clear expresion of the identity, dignity, and role of lay people in the mission of the Church. It is well written and well worth reading, but what does it all mean, and where does it take us?

The old negative definition of laity - those who do *not* share in the sacrament of orders - is no more, and we are now invited to see ourselves in terms of who and what we are, not in terms of what we lack. We learn that an active participation in Christ's saving work is not reserved for certain Christians with special education and training - it's the call to all of us through the sacraments of initiation. So if the call to holiness and mission is the common identity for clergy and laity alike, what then is the special lay perspective or experience we are to bring to the task? It is quite simply an understanding of how and where we are to carry out our call to share in Christ's mission.

One Mission - Different Callings

The call of the clergy is primarily but not exclusively to build up the Church, and the laity are invited to assist them in this task. If we look ahead 15-20 years, the assistance we will be called upon to give will be much more important than it is today.

In contrast to the primary call of the clergy, the main call of the laity is to bring the Gospel out into the secular world, and thereby to draw people into the Church. In our task we are to be assisted by the

clergy. Of course in many countries the laity are
needed to assist the clergy in building up the Church,
and we do this by undertaking special ministries and
services whenever necessary. But this work is neither the vision nor the primary task of mature laity
described in *Christifideles Laici* - here we are called
into the world. Perhaps part of our failure to answer
the call to go into the world is that lay people don't
feel we are sharing in Christ's mission *unless* we're
involved in a special Church ministry, committee, or
programme. So it is clear that much more must be
done to prepare us for our primary mission in the
world. We have a distorted image of lay spiritual
development which emphasises involvement in
Church ministry over action in the world. But the
mission of the Church is not her own renewal so
much as the evangelisation of the world. Pope Paul
VI clearly expressed this in *Evangelii Nuntiandi*,
when he said that the Church exists to evangelise.
We usually find, however, that priority is given to
the clerical ministry of building up the Church, making the lay calling in the world secondary. This naturally reinforces the old view that the clergy have a
higher calling than the laity. The correct way to see
it is as a *different* calling requiring special gifts, but
with the recognition that individual clergy and laity
are equal in God's sight.

Sacred or Secular?

To help us embrace the call to go into the world, we need to avoid a false distinction between the sacred and the secular. It's easy for us to look upon the Church as good, holy, and safe, while seeing the world as hostile, evil, and profane. This leads to a sense that we are living in a hostile world and retreating back to the safety of the Church. If this is the way we think, then we need to change, accepting God's view that creation is basically good, and sharing his love for the world. So our primary calling is to be labourers in the vineyard, presenting, promoting, and proclaiming the good news of salvation in Jesus to all those we meet. If we are to do this successfully, we need to be formed, equipped, and sent forth from our parish communities with a clear sense of value and commitment. For this we need a new partnership between clergy and laity, with each group understanding and living out their primary calling, whilst assisting each other whenever necessary. Our respective callings are not better or worse, they all demand commitment and sacrifices, but they are different.

A Brief Summary

So how does all this help us to fulfil our vocation and mission as lay faithful? 1.We need to recognise that baptism is the source of our identity and dignity, through which we are called to live holy lives, and lives of service. 2. We are called to take our place in the Church, putting our gifts at her disposal. 3. We are challenged to look outwards - to live the Gospel, to speak the Gospel, to make the Gospel present and thereby affect and change society. 4. We are reminded that there are a variety of vocations and callings, and that we must work together to build the Kingdom. For this to happen we need on-going formation and growth into maturity, so that we can use our gifts and carry out our mission. Therefore we are encouraged to form groups for spiritual renewal, and for John Paul II such groups are clear signs of the Holy Spirit at work in the Church, ful-filling the Second Vatican Council's vision of the Church as a community.

But the emphasis in *Christifideles Laici* is best summed up in the words "You go into my vineyard too". This call of the Lord is addressed to everyone, but in a particular way to the lay faithful, both men and women. So what are we waiting for?

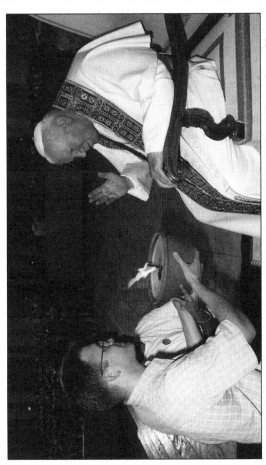

World Youth Day 15th August Jubilee 2000. John Paul II told Youth from all over the world: 'Do not be afraid to be the saints of the New Millennium.'

PRIESTHOOD IN THE TEACHING OF JOHN PAUL II

BY FR. PHILIP EGAN

One of Pope John Paul's favourite parables is the Parable of the Rich Young Man *(Mark 10: 17-22)*. It occurs throughout his writings, and notably in *Pastores Dabo Vobis* (hereafter *PDV*), the 1992 Apostolic Exhortation he issued about the formation of priests after the 1990 Synod of Bishops. It is a parable expressing the demands of Christian discipleship. But for the pope, this parable also says something about the qualities needed to be a priest today: total, radical self-giving. To be a priest today, it is not enough simply to know the Faith, the Gospel and the teaching of the Church. It is not enough even to be able to keep the Commandments, to live a virtuous life, to be a good person. You have to 'go over the top', that is, to make a complete self-sacrifice, to be madly in love with God, to give everything - all your energies, your heart, mind and imagination, your life and your all - to the love and service of Jesus Christ and his Church: "Go and sell everything you have, and give it to the poor ... then come, follow me."

The Pope's own specialisation is moral theology, but morals as set within anthropology, that is, within the study of the nature, condition and destiny of the human person. What does it mean to be human? How should human beings respond to the gift of existence? What should I do to be happy and fulfilled? His central message is that the only answer to the current malaise in world civilisation is Jesus Christ. Human beings can only attain true happiness in Jesus Christ, for "in the mystery of the Word made flesh" - as the Second Vatican Council put it, and as John Paul reminds us in his very first encyclical letter *Redemptor Hominis* - the "mystery of man truly becomes clear" (*Gaudium et Spes* 22). Jesus Christ not only reveals who God is: he reveals who we are. He is the Truth that sets us free, and the supreme model in himself of what it means to be fully human.

John Paul's 'theological anthropology' pervades his understanding of what it means to be a priest today. He has given considerable attention to the priesthood throughout his pontificate, notably in *Pastores Dabo Vobis*, already mentioned, and in *Gift and Mystery*, the book he wrote in 1996 to mark his Golden Jubilee of ordination. Moreover, after his election in 1978, he inaugurated the practice of writing an annual Letter to Priests on Holy Thursday, and these letters, now numbering more than twenty, form

an extensive compendium of his teaching. In 1993 he
focused on the priesthood in his Wednesday General
Audiences. He has also addressed in his pontificate
some of the controversial issues of the day such as
priestly celibacy and, in his 1994 Apostolic Letter
Ordinatio Sacerdotalis, the reservation of ordination
to the priesthood to men alone.

The Priesthood: new evangelization and martyrdom

In his writings about the priesthood, Pope John Paul
has brought his general theological vision to bear with
novel results. There are four points to make here.
First, John Paul has always been keenly aware of the
advent of the Third Millennium and the historic,
"momentous and fascinating times" in which we live.
This has given all his teaching, not least his understanding of priesthood, a missionary, evangelistic and
ecumenical slant. For John Paul, evangelisation and
humanisation - making all facets of our lives on earth
more authentically human - are really two sides of the
same coin. This is why he has constantly spoken of
the need for a new kind of evangelisation: an evangelisation "new in its methods, new in its fervour and
new in its expression" (cf. *Redemptoris Missio* 33).
This new evangelisation is directed to those places
and contexts such as the Western world, where the

initial fervour of the Gospel once proclaimed has now grown cool, and where many have lapsed or turned away from the faith. Moreover - and this is especially significant for priests - he sees evangelisation as intimately linked with sanctity, especially martyrdom. Since 1978, he has beatified over 1000 women and men and canonised over 400 new saints, many of whom were martyrs. The word 'martyr' means a witness and John Paul sees the martyr as the ideal Christian, the one who witnesses to the truth by laying down their life. As he wrote in one of his early poems: "The Word did not convert - but blood does".

Integral human liberation

Secondly, the Pope sees the work of priests as central to the promotion of Christian humanism. Here, his thought is akin to liberation theology, and is a reason why he has travelled so widely, undertaking many overseas journeys. His ambition has been to promote an "integral theology of human liberation" by challenging the various ideologies that threaten to overwhelm humans, to devalue human dignity and to smother human rights (cf. *Centesimus Annus* 26). In this he has given the lead to priests to do the same in their own contexts and situations. For John Paul, though, the root cause of the contemporary crisis is not unjust economic structures, poverty or the gulf between rich and poor:

these are the tragic symptoms. The root cause is the loss of the sense of God. When in 1995 he addressed the United Nations Assembly, he made an impassioned plea to the whole world to "respect the transcendent dimension of the human person" (*Address to the United Nations (1995)* 8). The loss of the sense of God has undermined certainty in knowledge and the foundations of ethics. This is why society today is facing a moral crisis: we find it increasingly difficult to grasp what it means to be human. Once the sense of God is lost, humans are torn adrift; they become prey to dangerous and tyrannical ideologies such as materialism and hedonism. People begin to exalt efficiency and productivity, rights rather than duties, the individual over and against the family and the community.

Engaging contemporary culture

Thirdly, John Paul wants priests to study and become engaged with contemporary culture. In the past, it would have been unthinkable for a pope to indulge in extensive overseas travels, to give TV interviews, or to play host to pop stars and media personalities. Some have said that John Paul wants to run the Church like a university seminar. Yet it is not the Catholic faith which has changed, but the world we live in. To facilitate a dialogue with it, we need therefore to study the world, to acquire an effective knowledge of it, to take an interest in science and contemporary culture (*Fides et Ratio* 43-4). In this way, the Church can bring about a great 'conversation' with every sector: the natural and human sciences, the arts, politics and economics, the communications media, psychology, literature, business and law. These vast areas need opening up to Christ so that they can hear the full truth about being human. John Paul sees the Church's role here as critical in a positive and a negative sense. Christians are called to be witnesses, "the people of life for life", called to offer humanity the liberating Gospel of life (*Evangelium Vitae* 78-9). Yet we must not underestimate the great struggle going on between the culture of life and the culture of death discernible in the growing trivialisation of the value of life through abortion, the killing of the innocent, murder, embryo experimentation and euthanasia.

Hope of the young

And fourthly, John Paul is concerned about the young, and it is the young whom he encourages priests to become especially concerned with.

People who have had supper with the Pope in recent years have noticed on his sideboard just one photograph: a photograph of himself in a helicopter about to land in Cherry Creek State Park, Denver Colorado, for the 1993 World Youth Day, with over half a million youngsters awaiting him below. The institution in 1985 of a bi-annual World Youth Day has been one of the great features of his pontificate, yet everyone was saying that Denver would be a flop. This was not a traditionally Catholic country like Poland or the Philippines but a modern secular city, with all the usual problems of drugs, crime and family breakdown. No-one would come, they said: American youth are materialistic, bored with religion, at odds with Church's teaching on sex and everything else. Yet as things turned out, the visit to Denver was one of John Paul's happiest memories, what he later dubbed "the great surprise"; however modern and secular, the young, he declared, had not outgrown the need for religious faith.

Why the young? Because the "future of the world and the Church belongs to the young" (*Tertio Millennio Adveniente* 58). John Paul's theology is about hope, and hope is exactly what he sees in the young. Youth is a special moment in life when ideals flourish, when identity and vocation forms, and when the first serious personal decisions are made. Like the Rich Young Man in the parable, young people need guidance; they have a natural generosity and radicalism, an idealism not yet tainted by the cares of life or the cynicism and comfort-seeking of middle-age. This is why they need priests to guide them. The Church, ever missionary, he says, must go out to meet the new generations, who "seem to be accepting with enthusiasm what their elders have rejected" (*Crossing the Threshold of Hope*, p. 113). God is preparing a new springtime for the Gospel. The Holy Spirit is even now influencing individuals, societies and cultures, histories and religions, raising up ideals and aspirations for a more noble world, sowing seeds of the Word and preparing people for the Gospel. The Pope sees grounds for this hope in the young people of the world, and also in the various movements for justice, peace, development, the rights of minorities, feminism, and ecology.

Development of Doctrine

These four themes - of new evangelisation and martyrdom, of integral human liberation, of the Church as being like a seminar engaged with culture, and the pervasive sense of hope centred on the young - shape John Paul's understanding of what it means to be a priest and give being a priest new vision.

Priests have had a bad press in recent times. The social status of priesthood within contemporary culture has diminished. Moreover, some have noted that where Vatican II gave a renewed clarity to the function of bishops and laity in the Church, as well as reviving the diaconate, it said relatively little about the priesthood. Certainly in the welter of change occurring within the Church in the period after the Council a crisis of priestly identity has arisen. Theologically far-reaching questions have been asked about the language of priesthood and its foundations in scripture. What is a priest? Is his identity defined by his being or by what he does? What is the exact distinction between the priesthood and lay ministry? Can we explore other models of leadership for today's circumstances? In view of the shortage of priests in many parts of the world, might we consider ordaining married men, or the ordination of women, or the 'temporary' ordination of suitable lay people to lead the Eucharist?

John Paul has therefore given special attention to the theology of priesthood, especially in *Pastores Dabo Vobis*, which forms a magnificent compendium of his teaching on priesthood, and in which he attempts to tackle some of the major issues to do with priestly identity. On the one hand, he has drawn renewed attention to the documents of Vatican II which state that whilst the whole Church is a priestly people, the hierarchical or ministerial priesthood (of bishops and priests) and the common priesthood (of the laity) participate in Christ's priesthood each in their own distinctive way. Ordered one to the other, they differ in essence and degree (*Lumen Gentium* 10). The Council also taught that within the ministerial

priesthood, there are two degrees of participation: the
episcopacy, which enjoys the fullness of order, and the
presbyterate, those who are fellow-workers with the
bishops. Finally, the Council speaks of deacons.
Deacons are sacramentally ordained and assist the
bishops and priests. There are thus three grades within
the Sacrament of Holy Order: bishops, priests and deacons. But the term priesthood (Latin *sacerdos*) is
reserved to bishops and priests (cf. *Catechism of the
Catholic Church,* 1554-71).

Yet John Paul has done more than simply repeat
the doctrine of Vatican II. He has developed it and
given it a new vision in the light of his own theological orientation. In the key paragraphs 11 to 18 of
Pastores Dabo Vobis, he speaks of the identity of the
priest as dynamic and relational, since his identity
has its source in the Blessed Trinity. Just as the
Church herself is a "mystery of Trinitarian communion in missionary tension" so too the priest "sacramentally enters into communion with the Bishop and
other priests" in order to serve God's people and to
draw all to Christ *(PDV, 12).* The priest is thus a "living and transparent image of Christ the Priest", not
only "in the Church but also in the forefront of the
Church" *(PDV, 16).* John Paul's Trinitarian emphasis
gives new vigour to the traditional three-fold mission
of the priest as one configured to Christ the Priest,

Prophet and Shepherd. He speaks instead of the priest as the servant of the mystery, communion and mission of the Church. The priest is one who makes present the risen Christ through celebrating the sacraments; he builds up the unity of the Church's communion, and he helps that community to become the herald of and witness to the Gospel.

For John Paul, the priest is called to be a martyr, an evangelist, an ecumenist, a man of the sacred whose life speaks louder than his words, and who, prolonging the presence of Christ, embodies his way of life (*PDV,* 15). Placed "at the forefront of the Church", he is called to live a nuptial relationship with her, like Christ the bridegroom who laid down his life for his Bride the Church (*PDV,* 22). The priest is to be a father, especially to the young, their companion in tourism, sports and cultural interests, a good listener, able, like Christ in the Parable of the Rich Young Man, to offer guidance on the fundamental issues of life. He is to preach human liberation, calling everyone to respect the transcendent dimension of the human person. His mission is to engage in dialogue with all people of good will, and especially with contemporary culture, to open it up to Christ and the Gospel. If he is to do this, he has to become a student of the world we live in, a man of hope supporting all those movements that contribute to authentic humanism.

Priestly Spirituality

The exact nature of priestly spirituality has been much discussed in recent times. For John Paul, three aspects are important.

First, priesthood has to be marked by a spirit of self-sacrificing service, the "gift of self, the total gift of self to the Church, following the example of Christ" (*PDV,* 23). The ministerial priesthood for John Paul is not about power, but service: in representing Christ who in his priestly self-sacrifice on Calvary showed himself to be the "one who came not to be served but to serve" *(Mark 10:45).* Moreover, throughout his writings on the priesthood, he stresses that the ordained priesthood is at the service of the general priesthood of the laity, that is, the priest is the one who has to identify and release the gifts of the laity in order to put them at the service of the Gospel. He has never been a clericalist: even in his younger days as a priest and bishop, his mind-set and attitudes were often unconventional. In *Christifideles Laici,* he says along with traditional theology, that the priest by ordination acts *in persona Christi,* in the person of Christ, but he adds: *in persona Christi Capitis et Pastoris,* in the person of Christ the Head and Shepherd. This fits in exactly with his theology of gender and sexuality: that women are the most important members of the Church because they represent the Marian dimension. The Petrine ministry within the Church exists to serve the Marian. In his 1995 *Letter to Priests*, he argues that women have a special role in the Church's mission. Priests should treat women as true sisters, finding ways to help them realise their vocation of sharing in the work of Christ, the Priest, Prophet and Shepherd. Moreover, in his 1995 *Letter to Women*, he notes that women have a special role in humanisation: they help everyone recover the Marian dimension of anthropology, the primacy of the contemplative over the active, an awareness of receptivity, gratitude and wonder challenging male overemphasis on efficiency and productivity.

Secondly, evangelical transparency and celibacy. The *sine qua non* for being a priest today, especially in affluent Western consumer-cultures, is, the pope argues, evangelical transparency and simplicity: 'this man, by the way he lives, acts and thinks, reminds people of Jesus'. *Pastores Dabo Vobis* speaks of the "radicalism of the Gospel" and the ethical demand this makes on the priest *(PDV, 27)*. Moreover, priestly service, availability and self-sacrifice is fittingly expressed in the Western Church, John Paul avers, by the charism and discipline of celibacy. Celibacy is a "personal gift" of the priest to Jesus and his Church that "prefigures and anticipates the perfect and final communion and self-giving of the world to come" *(PDV, 29)*. The priest imitates the celibacy of Christ and just as Christ laid down his life for his Bride the Church, so too the priest.

And thirdly, priests must be prophetic. A priest is configured by his ordination to Christ the Priest, Prophet and Shepherd, yet for John Paul, it is the 'prophet dimension', the priest as Minister of the Word, that is paramount. It's interesting that in one of his Wednesday General Audiences, he spoke of priests not just having one day off a week, but two: i.e. a second day for prayer, reflection and study. This would help the priest in his work of writing, publishing, and being involved with the TV, radio, media and local cultural sectors. John Paul sees the priest as being like the pope to the world, not only the Servant of the People of God, but the servant of all humanity: the visible face of the Catholic Church in the culture, community and context in which he works. This is not, of course, to secularise the priest or take over the laity's role but rather so that the priest can support the laity in their engagement with the secular world for the spread of the Gospel.

Priests for Tomorrow

In reading Pope John Paul's writings, one quickly realises that he is in himself, his life and example, probably the best model of the noble and uplifting vision of priesthood he puts forward. It is a vision of priesthood thoroughly evangelistic in outlook and one that will undoubtedly have important implications for seminary training in the years ahead. In *Pastores Dabo Vobis*, the pope speaks about the basic human and relational qualities needed to be a priest today; he suggests the need for a pre-seminary year of spiritual and human formation where helpful. He also proposes that students for the priesthood be helped to read the signs of the times by studying the human sciences - sociology, psychology, educational theory, literature, economics and politics - in order to come to grips with the culture into which they will be sent as evangelisers.

At the end of *Pastores Dabo Vobis*, John Paul calls on the entire Church to "pray and work tirelessly for priestly vocations", appealing to parents to be generous and to young people to be docile to the Spirit's voice *(PDV, 82)*. He turns to Mary, the Mother of Priests, the one "human being who responded better than any other to God's call" to seek her prayers. We might fittingly do the same at the end of this reflection and make John Paul's Marian prayer for priests our own:

"Accept those who have been called.
Protect their growth and their life ministry;
O Mother of priests, accompany your sons."

THE SOCIAL TEACHING
OF JOHN PAUL II

BY RODGER CHARLES SJ

John Paul II has brought to maturity the modern social teaching of the Church which developed from *Rerum Novarum* of Leo XIII (1891) - though there were social encyclicals before that and the social teaching tradition goes back to the scriptures. That he should be Pope at the end of the disastrous 20th century when that social teaching became so important was singularly a blessing to the Church and the world. Living under the Nazis from 1939 he, like all Poles went in fear of his life and in order to escape their clutches, while studying clandestinely for the priesthood, he worked as a quarryman for four years. From 1945 under the Communists he had to face a more subtle but no less real persecution of a people. Such experiences made him determined to proclaim above all the human dignity which he had seen so violated under these totalitarianisms. *Redemptor Hominis*, '*The redeemer of man*' (1979), his first encyclical, (and first encyclicals contain the essence of a particular

Pope's agenda) deals with the theological foundations of human dignity, Christ as the perfect man, who restored in the children of Adam, the likeness of God. "By his incarnation, he, the son of God, has in a certain way, united himself with each man. He worked with human hands, he thought with a human mind, acted with a human will and with a human heart he loved" *(RH 8)*. All then should be treated justly as brothers and sisters of Christ.

A Social Teaching rooted in experience

As a young man he was early interested in problems of social justice, and the social teaching of the Church as a way of building a new and better Poland. Gifted as actor, writer, poet, linguist and dramatist, his intention was to pursue a career in the arts. He was also an active man enjoying soccer, skiing, canoeing and mountaineering with his friends. When, in 1941 the war turned his mind to priesthood, his further gifts as theologian and philosopher surfaced. Doctoral and postdoctoral studies in these subjects followed. As a priest he did a great deal of pastoral work which he loved. Men and women, young and old, the prosperous and those less so, all found in him a friend always. He was still active as writer, playwright and poet and had the widest range of friends in the arts, the sciences, and the professions. He became

Professor of Social Ethics at Lublin in 1956, was Bishop in 1958, Archbishop in 1964 and Cardinal in 1967. A key figure in the Second Vatican Council, he greatly influenced the drafting of *Gaudium et Spes* and *Dignitatis Humanae*, the two documents concerned with justice in society and human rights.

Liberation Theology

As Pope, one of the first tasks he had to face was the burgeoning of liberation theology, in Latin America especially. At the Latin American Bishops Council (CELAM) at Puebla Mexico in January 1979 it was a central issue. A valid and necessary concept in itself, some naively thought liberation could be combined with baptizing Marx and adopting his social analysis. John Paul was not impressed. He had pondered, and rejected, the use of violence in search of social justice as a young dramatist working on the life of St. Albert - a 19th century Pole who worked with the poor, while his close acquaintance with real socialism revealed it for the disaster it was. On January 19th 1979 he told the Mexican priests and religious they were not political leaders but men of God, centres of unity in the Church. Addressing the Bishops the next day, he stressed that *the truth about Christ* does not warrant any interpretation of his life as that of the social revolutionary from Nazareth. *The truth about the Church* is that her mission is to proclaim to all the kingdom of Christ, not just to one social class. *The truth about man* is that the primordial anthropology of Genesis does not accommodate the idea of him as a mere fragment of nature for he is made in God's image. Two days later he addressed half a million Indios in Cuilapan announcing himself as the champion of those poor who knew much of deprivation. That he had himself had experience of backbreaking labour that did not render the necessities of a truly decent life made his heart go out to them and their loved ones. Justice must be done, the necessary reforms must be put in place. Then in Poland in June 1979, he began that process of encouraging his fellow country men to insist on recognition of their human dignity and their right to freedom, and to do so peacefully, which miraculously would ten years later enable them to claim it.

The Social Encyclicals

John Paul II has issued three strictly social encyclicals but the message of human rights and social justice has been at the heart of all his pastoral visits across the world while many of his other encyclicals and official documents touch on the same. To *Redemptor Hominis* we have already referred. *Dives in misericodia* shows the need for love as well as justice in dealing with social problems, the Apostolic Constitution

Familiaris Consortio (1981) and the Apostolic Letter
Mulieris Dignitatem (1998) deal with the family,
which is the basis of state and church, and the dignity
of women respectively, while *Veritatis Splendor* and
Evangelium Vitae show how basic sound moral values
are to a just society.

Laborem Exercens

Laborem Exercens his first social encyclical is the
most comprehensive and coherent in depth treat-
ment given to any one particular aspect of the
Church's social teaching. His own experience of
hard manual work taught him to reflect deeply on
these things in the light of the scriptures. The
encyclical starts by reminding us that man is placed
in the world by God to work it and so earn his daily
bread, it is a mark of his role as a person. The
Church took up the cause of the workers in *Rerum
Novarum* (1891) and this new encyclical document
is one with it *(LE 1-3)* In working, man imitates his
creator *(LE 4)* and in God's plan work is always
personal, subjective, done by one who is a person,
conscious of that. Work as objective *(LE 5)*, its end
product, is important and as such it is valued in different ways, but whatever honest work a man does,
however humble, gives him human dignity which
demands respect. We do not value people by what

they do. We value them and their work by what they are, sons and daughters of God *(LE 6)*. The liberal capitalist in the 19th century did not do this *(LE 7)* and the workers' reaction in solidarity was justified *(LE 8)*.Work is sometimes hard, this is the penalty that sin placed on man and the Christian will join his suffering in this to those of his master Christ. Industriousness meanwhile is a moral habit which makes man good *(LE 9)*.

Liberal capitalism produced the Marxist reaction and the theory of social revolution leading to communism, so opposing capital and labour *(LE 11)*. But while the church teaches that labour has priority over capital, capital and labour cannot be opposed *(LE 13)* the production process emphasizes this. The only legitimate title to the possession of goods, private or public however is their service of labour. Proposals for enabling wage earners to share in management, ownership or profits are therefore significant .in this context *(LE 14)*.

The more personal approach to the relationship between capital and labour, and the rights of and obligations of labour are then considered *(LE 15)*. Direct and indirect employers must do their part in providing the conditions in which these can be secured. The worker has a right and a duty to work *(LE 17-18)*, to adequate wages and conditions *(LE 19)*, to organize in trade unions working for justice constructively, in a spirit of solidarity not class egoism *(LE 20)*.

Sollicitudo Rei Socialis

Sollicitudo Rei Socialis (1987) reminds us that it is part of an updated *corpus* of documents built up since Leo XIII *(SRS 1)*. It deals with the way in which the universal purpose of created things is achieved by economic justice between nations *(SRS 5-10)*. When Paul VI published his *Populorum Progressio* in 1977, there was more optimism about overcoming the problems of world poverty in all its aspects *(SRS 12)*. The blame for later pessimism rests on rich and poor nations alike. The rich for operating economic, financial and social mechanisms which often penalize the poorer, while the elites in less developed countries have too often failed in doing what they could and should do to help their country's self development *(SRS 16)*. Problems are caused by the conflicts between the power blocs and by the failure to come to terms with demographic changes *(SRS 19-25)*. There are however positive signs, for example the growing awareness of human rights, of the respect for life itself in face of abortion or euthanasia, the concern for the environment and for peace and justice *(SRS 26)*.

There are also the moral problems of economic development. In itself it is a good and a necessary process. But it should not mean over development, which harms the environment, moral as well as physical, while leading to consumerism *(SRS 27-30)*. We should not despair of solving these problems, but with faith in God, and with co-operation between peoples and respect for human rights, solidarity and respect for our world, seek answers *(SRS 31-34)*. In fact there has been and is selfishness, lack of vision and moral principle; it is right to speak of structures of sin caused by excessive concentration on profit and power. Conversion of heart alone is the answer to these,.it leads to true solidarity; those with economic power should use that power justly while those without it do what they can for the common good, being neither passive nor threatening to destroy the social fabric *(SRS 35-38)*. Peace is the work of justice and, by extension, of solidarity. The Church tries to give moral guidance. It is not in her remit to recommend or enact specific political or economic solutions or systems. She will condemn the evils she sees; but more positively she will try to support policies that are aimed at real solutions, just solutions *(SRS 41- 45)*. Liberation theology which respects the values set out in the documents of the social magisterium (eg *Libertatis Conscientia*), will help in this. Solidarity is above all solidarity with the poor *(SRS 46-49)*.

Centesimus Annus

The collapse of the Soviet monolith began in 1989, just before the one hundredth anniversary of *Rerum Novarum*, which required special commemoration. This came in 1991 with John Paul II's encyclical *Centesimus Annus*, 'On the hundredth anniversary' of Leo XIII's *Rerum Novarum* in which the Pope guided a Catholic Church in Europe and the USA, confused about how to respond to liberal capitalism. He condemned its excesses. He also condemned the Communist idea of the social ownership of productive goods, only economic freedom will provide the wealth with which their needs will be met. He was remarkably prescient. It was the inability of the Marxist command economy to meet the needs of the people that lay behind its rejection by the people, but until the 1970s that seemed a long way away.

In the meantime since 1917, the world had been racked by tensions between the two systems; many Westerners perversely thought the Communist system best, though they carefully avoided living under it. When in the 1980s it became apparent that the monolith was imploding the only question was, would it do so peacefully or in violence? It is here that John Paul's experience, wisdom and knowledge, put the world forever in his debt because it was the lead he gave to his fellow countrymen in reclaiming civil society peacefully, by insisting on human rights and responsibilities, that finally by 1989 had sapped the strength of Polish Communism and so gave the example to others that it could all be done with minimal violence.

Some said that the collapse of the Soviet system marked the end of history. It was not of course, but it was the end of the debate on what was the best social system. It is one in which, personal, social, political and economic freedom existed. Sadly Western freedom in fact is severely defective as *Centesinus Annus* points out.

It takes *Rerum Novarum* as the starting point *(CA 1-10)*. That document centred on the dignity of man and the State's duty to the common good in responsible freedom *(CA 11)*. Today there is still need in some circumstances to face conflict in the search for justice, but not the Marxist way *(CA 14)*. The world rejected the totalitarian Communist system from 1989, peaceful Poland showing the way *(CA 22-24)*. We must look to the future, not looking for a perfect social system; self interest must be harmonized with the common good otherwise bureaucracy stifles freedom *(CA 25)*. The earth was given to all and all must share its wealth. This is done primarily by work and that means know-how, technology and skill, foreseeing the needs of others, and supplying those needs at a just price in a free, morally responsible market *(CA 30-31)*. All

must have access to the market and many through
poverty do not; individuals and countries must be
given that access by those who are fortunate to have it
themselves *(CA 33-34)*. If this is done the free market
is most efficient in use of resources *(CA 33)*. Profit is
a good if it is a measure of that efficiency, achieved
with human and moral needs respected *(CA 35)*.

In the third world especially conditions are often as
bad as in the nineteenth century. Unions must seek
justice, not for socialism which has failed, but 'a society of free work, enterprise and participation in which
meets the needs of the whole society. Capitalism as
we know it is not the only alternative *(CA 35)*. That
brand of capitalism produces consumerism. It does
not distinguish between needs which foster, and needs
which undermine, the human person so that evils e.g.
drugs are seen as goods. It is not wrong to live better;
it is wrong to make goods an end in themselves *(CA
36)*. Consumerism ravages the physical and moral
environment, marriage and family especially *(CA 37-
9)*. Economic life has become absolutized; the market
becomes the subject of idolatry. Economic freedom is
only one aspect of freedom which must primarily be
spiritual and religious *(CA 40)*.

Western society is alienated as its work system
and its members use one another in the pursuit of
wealth and mass communications manipulate them

(CA 41). Is then capitalism the model for the world? It is better to say the market economy, private owner-ship of productive goods, business creativity. In a strong juridical framework at the service of human freedom, the core of which is ethical and religious is the model *(CA 41)*. In fact the danger now is of a rad-ical ideology, of freedom that knows no restraint *(CA 42)*. What we should be seeing is an ownership of the means of production that serves useful work; that is their purpose *(CA 43)*.

The political system must be based on freedom, but modern democracy, which rejects the idea of ultimate truth leads to totalitarianism; absolute val-ues which safeguard human rights alone protect true freedom *(CA 44-46)*. In pursuit of the common good the state should foster the conditions which produce a sound market system. It can intervene to prevent poverty and deprivation by helping people to get out of them but a social assistance state is self defeat-ing. Voluntary services however foster self help *(CA 48)*. The Church has a role in helping to create soli-darity and charity *(CA 49-52)* . Her message enrich-es human dignity *(CA 55)*, it stresses the preferential option for the poor. The solution to national prob-lems lies in the cooperation which liberal capitalism and Marxism rejected *(CA 60)*. The world is more aware today of the need for religious values in

reform and the Church knows that Almighty God
has given his Church to lead man into the third millenium, along with Christ her Lord and Mary his
mother in a pilgrimage of faith *(CA 62)*.

Bringing the Social Teaching to its maturity

He has done this in three ways. In the first place he has
woven the foundation principle of Catholic social teaching - that man, redeemed by Christ, is the purpose and
end of every social organization - so firmly into the
social teaching of the Church that it has been given a
new and a needed coherence. At Puebla he rejected the
illusions of a Christian Marxism, while insisting that the
deep set problems of poverty cry to heaven and must be
addressed with the vigour their urgency demands. In
Laborem Exercens he showed the dignity of work and
worker which Liberal capitalism and Marxism both
denied, and which capitalism today has not fully accepted. *Sollicitudo Rei Socialis* emphasized the failure of the
richer nations to do their part fully to see that all
mankind have access to the means to gain an adequate
livelihood and of the elites in the poorer nations whom
too often have not accepted their social responsibilities.

Secondly in *Centesimus Annus* he responded not
to the end of history, but to the end of the illusion
that we can build a perfect social system; we will not
get one here on earth and attempts to do so crucify

man made in God's image as did national socialism and the Marxist variety.

Thirdly while stressing that the morally operating free or market economy best serves the common good, he stresses that the Western capitalist variety is seriously defective. Under it not all have access to the market, and they must get it. In capitalism as we know it, consumerism, making goods an end in themselves, is an evil corrupting the physical and human environment. There has to be state action according to the principle of subsidiarity to assist those suffering poverty to recover from it and become independent again. However a social assistance state is not the answer. Democracy becomes totalitarian if it is not based on objective moral values. It is because capitalist democracies are not so based they become cultures of death - of contraception, abortion and euthanasia as *Veritatis Splendor* and *Evangelium Vitae* show.

John Paul II's life experience has included struggles with poverty, against Nazism and Communism and these gave him the soundest credentials in developing the social teaching of the Church, while his wide and profound learning uniquely enabled him to do so with consummate skill. A pontificate with so many triumphs for Christ and his Church has none greater than this. One of her greatest treasures, and surely the most neglected until now, is at last fully at her service.

WOMEN IN THE TEACHING
OF JOHN PAUL II

BY MICHELE M. SCHUMACHER

Far from measuring the dignity and vocation of
women according to a male standard - an accusation
commonly launched by traditional feminism against a
patriarchical society in general and a male hierarchy
in particular - John Paul II presents this significant
and timely subject within the light of Christ, the Son
of God and the Son of Mary. In his apostolic letter on
women (*Mulieris dignitatem*; henceforth *MD*), he
takes as his own the Second Vatican Council's presentation of Christ as fully revealing the human person to himself or herself and of making his (her)
"supreme calling clear" (*MD 2*; cf. *Gaudium et spes*
22). This revelation of the human person - man *and*
woman - by Christ is, John Paul II continues (with
further reference to the Council), accomplished in the
definitive revelation of his communion with the
Father and the Spirit: "The Lord Jesus, when he
prayed to the Father 'that all may be one... as we are
one' *(Jn 17:21.22)*, opened up vistas closed to human

reason. For he implied *a certain likeness* between the union of the divine Persons and the union of God's children in truth and charity. This likeness reveals that man, who is the only creature on earth which God willed for its own sake, cannot fully find himself except through a sincere gift of self" (cf. *MD 7*; cf. *Gaudium et spes 24 and MD 30*).

The Foundation of Women's Dignity: The Divine Image and Likeness

In both his Marian year meditation on the dignity and vocation of women, *Mulieris dignitatem* (written in 1988), and his reflection on "the problems and the prospects of what it means to be a woman in our time," his "*Letter to Women*" (written on the occasion of the Beijing Conference in 1995; henceforth *LW*), John Paul II addresses as essential and even "indispensable" *(MD 7)* a God-centered vision of the human person. Commenting upon Genesis 1:27 - "God created man in his own image, in the image of God he created him; male and female he created them" - the pope notes that the divine image in human persons - in men and women equally - is constituted by their rational nature whereby they are capable of knowing and loving God *(MD 7)* and in virtue of which - even in spite of historical conditioning - they are able to recognize the intrinsic dignity of all human persons (although the pontiff highlights that of women; see *LW 6*). Beyond this, the second account of creation *(Gen 2:18-25)* - which the pontiff recognizes as "a prelude to the definitive self - revelation of the Triune God" - points to the relational significance of the human person's likeness to God. Because man cannot exist "alone" *(Gen 2:18)*, his likeness to God "also involves existing in a relationship, in relation to the other 'I'" *(MD 7)*. This relationship is, moreover - and the pope insists - "mutual": woman is related to man, but man is also related to woman. Woman complements man, but man also complements woman; and this is the case on the physical and psychological levels, of course, but also and especially on the ontological level (i.e. that of the complete being). In their "interpersonal community," they form a "unity of the two," a "uni-duality," which preserves the "specific diversity and personal originality" of both *(LW 7-8; MD 7, 10)*. Theirs is a relationship of mutual "being 'for' the other" *(MD 7)*, of "mutual giving at the service of love and life" *(LW 2)*. The Creator's entrusting of each to the other requires that both man and woman be responsible for the other's self-gift *(MD 14)*. Hence the Pauline exhortation that "wives be subject to your husbands, as to the Lord" *(Eph 5:22)* must be understood as a *"mutual subjection out of reverence for Christ"* and not just that of the wife to the husband" (*MD 24* with reference to *Eph 5:21*).

This "innovation of the Gospel" points to just one of the established cultural norms which, the pope insists, must be transformed in imitation of Christ and in response to his Gospel. Historical condition has, he admits, posed a serious obstacle to the legitimate progress of women. Often "relegated to the margins of society and reduced to servitude," women have not been permitted to be their authentic selves, and this, in turn, has resulted in the "spiritual impoverishment of all of humanity" *(LW 3)*. To the extent, on the other hand, that history has unfolded according to the divine plan for the human race - according to the "principle of mutually being 'for' the other" - there is a harmonious "integration of *what is 'masculine' and what is 'feminine'*" *(MD 7)*.

Two Dimensions of Women's Vocation:
Maternal and Virginal Self-Giving

This giving of oneself to the other so as to actually *be* 'for' the other enables man and woman "to discover their humanity ever anew and to confirm its whole meaning" *(MD 7)*. This fundamental affirmation of woman's dignity which - not unlike that of man - is founded in her creation in the divine image, indicates, the pope teaches, the "ethical dimension" of her vocation: *"Woman can only find herself by giving love to others" (MD 30)*. Certainly God willed the human person - each and every person - for himself or herself. On the other hand, to be a person means "striving towards self-realization," and this, John Paul II continues, is achieved *"through a sincere gift of self" (MD 7)*. It follows, according to the papal teaching, that the image of God in the human person is both a gift and a task. This distinction between created and achieved perfection (which is founded upon the classical philosophical distinction according to which the nature of a being determines its operation, which in turn determines the means of its perfection) founds the further distinction between dignity and vocation. "A woman's dignity is closely connected," the pope teaches, "with the love which she receives by the very reason of her femininity; it is likewise connected *with the love which she gives in return" (MD 30)*.

Here reference is made to the spousal nature of woman's vocation which is necessarily shared *by* the man, (he too is called to become a gift for the other) but not necessarily *with him*: it refers "not only or above all to the specific spousal relationship of marriage. It means something more universal..." *(MD 29; cf. n. 7)*. Marriage and consecrated celibacy - which are likewise expressed with reference to the fruit that they bear as physical and spiritual motherhood - are, the pope remarks, two "faces" of the fundamental and universal vocation to love God and neighbour, to become a gift for the other *(MD 17, cf. LW 12)*. Even the marital vocation should, however, be an expression, or form, of the more fundamental vocation to offer one's life to the divine Bridegroom. Holiness, the pope teaches, consists precisely in this *(see MD 22)*. In keeping, moreover, with the fundamental insight that woman *"receives love in order to love in return" (MD 29)*, the bridal vocation is necessarily linked to the maternal *(see MD 18)*.

The human being is entrusted by God "in a special way," maintains John Paul II, to woman *(MD, 30)*. In the first instance, this entrusting refers to her physical maternity whereby her femininity is made manifest: woman is revealed as the one in whom human life is conceived and developed. "The 'woman,' as mother and first teacher of the human being (education being the spiritual dimension of parenthood), has a special precedence over the man," the pope claims *(MD, 19)*. This initial and fundamental meaning of the entrusting of humanity to women points to and fosters the characteristic openness of women to human persons in general. The pope speaks of the unique contact between a mother and her child as giving rise to a certain attitude of attentiveness with regard to all human persons. This, he continues, constitutes the particular "genius" of women, which is that of ensuring a "sensitivity for human beings in every circumstance" *(MD 30; cf. 18; LW 12).*

The Prophetic Character of Femininity and the Order of Love

Commenting upon the Letter to the Ephesians *(5:21-33),* the pope notes that the analogy between Christ and the Church, on the one hand, and the Bridegroom and the Bride, on the other, clarifies *"what is decisive for the dignity of women...* In God's eternal plan, woman is the one in whom the order of love in the created world of persons takes first root" *(ibid.).* In so doing - in receiving the love of the Bridegroom (who, in accord with the biblical analogy, is purposefully ambiguous so as to be potentially both Christ and her own husband; cf. *MD 25)* - she is, so to speak, *enabled* to love: to become a gift for the other. In accord with the biblical analogy, she *"receives love, in order to love in return"* so as also to manifest the *"order of love"*: the dynamism of giving and receiving, proper to "intimate life" of the Triune God, which is communicated to human persons through the Holy Spirit. Within this context, the pope addresses a certain *"'prophetic' character of women in their femininity."* Precisely as women - as "brides" - they manifest, "in the context of the biblical analogy and the text's interior logic,... the love with which every human being - man and woman - is loved by God in Christ" *(MD 29)*. Hence, although the Church, as Bride, is "*a collective subject* and not *an individual person*," in her, every human being is called to become the bride of Christ by accepting the gift of his redemptive love and by responding to it "with the gift of his or her own person" *(MD 25)*.

This bridal role of the faithful - of men as well as women - constitutes, within the papal vision, the baptismal priesthood to which are all called. United to Christ, the divine Bridegroom, by a "sincere gift" of self - a gift which is necessarily a response to him who loved us "first" *(cf. 1 Jn 4:19)* - she, the Bride who is present in each of the faithful, shares in his life and his threefold mission (priestly, prophetic and kingly). The "very essence of the Church" as a community consecrated to Christ (as his bride) is nonetheless symbolically present, John Paul II teaches, in women, and more especially in faithful women. Theirs is an "inherent 'prophecy' ... , a highly significant 'iconic character,' which finds its full realization in Mary" *(LW 11)*.

This prophetic character of women in their femininity is obviously realized in the context of a relationship: it is the divine Bridegroom who reveals her to herself and to the world. Thus, although the pope refers to the

Spirit's mission of introducing human persons into the Trinitarian life and thus into the "order of love" *(MD 29)*, he particularly emphasizes the role of Christ. It is he, the divine Bridegroom, who offers a "sincere gift" of himself: his body has been "given," his blood has been "poured out" as a gift for the beloved *(cf. Lk 22:19-22; Eph 5:25-27)*. By this redeeming act which "gives definitive prominence to the spousal meaning of God's love," he creates the Church, his bride and body, and simultaneously unites her to himself "as the bridegroom with the bride" *(MD 26)*.

Corresponding to the prophetic character of women in their femininity is thus the iconic character of man in his masculinity. It is precisely this sexual distinction - in virtue of which man and woman together form a "sacrament" of the relationship between Christ and the Church *(cf. Eph 5)* - that the man is, according to the papal argument, a fitting minister *("in persona Christi")* of the sacraments *(MD 26)*. The Eucharist, which "realizes anew" the spousal act of Christ is, the pope teaches, *"the Sacrament of the Bridegroom and of the bride" (MD 26). "The symbol of the Bridegroom is masculine,"* and appropriately so, for Christ is, the pope insists, "true man, a male" *(MD 25)*. The distinction of roles within the sacramental economy is thus "in no way prejudicial to women," for it is "an expres-

sion of what is specific to being male and female"
and not an "arbitrary imposition" *(LW 11)*.

Mary, the "New Beginning" of the Dignity and Vocation of Women

The biblical vision of reality accords no adequate
explanation "of what is 'human,'" observes John Paul
II, without appropriate reference to what is 'feminine.'
Analogically within the economy of salvation: "we
cannot omit, in the perspective of our faith, the mystery of 'woman': virgin - mother - spouse" *(MD 22)*. If
the dignity and vocation of women is indeed
"revealed" in the mystery of the Incarnate Word - to
return to John Paul II's initial and fundamental insight
from whence we shall draw our conclusion - then
"Woman - Mother of God" determines, he maintains,
"the essential horizon" of this reflection. "The dignity
of every human being and the vocation corresponding
to that dignity find their definitive measure in *union
with God" (MD 5)*. She, the *Theotokos* (God-bearer),
"fulfills in the most eminent manner the supernatural
predestination to union with the Father" *(MD 4)* to
which all human persons are called. This predestination which is accomplished by her free and personal
cooperation (her *fiat*) simultaneously inaugurates the
New Covenant to be definitively accomplished in the
sacrificial offering of Christ's body and blood which

he receives from her *(cf. MD 19)*. The "representative" and the "archetype of the whole human race" *(MD 4)*, the Virgin - Mother of Christ is also, the pope teaches, "'the new beginning' of the *dignity and vocation of women*, of each and every woman" *(MD 11)*.

THE THEOLOGY OF THE BODY: AN EDUCATION IN BEING HUMAN

BY CHRISTOPHER WEST

What if I told you that the key to understanding God's plan for human life is to go behind the fig leaves and behold the human body, naked and without shame? What if I told you that the only way to see the invisible mystery of God is through the vision of the human body in its masculinity and femininity? What if I told you that the Christian mystery itself is simply unintelligible unless we understand the meaning of sexual difference and our call to sexual union?

You would probably think I was a bit obsessed with sex and naked bodies. You might even think I've been corrupted by our pagan, pornographic culture. Understandable. But what if Pope John Paul II were telling you these things?

Indeed, these - among other things - are what we learn from the first major catechetical project of John Paul II's pontificate known as the "theology of the body." In this collection of 129 audience addresses delivered between September 1979 and November 1984, John Paul developed what promises to be one of his most enduring and important contributions to the Church and the world.

The theology of the body is a scriptural reflection on the human experience of embodiment connected as it is with erotic desire and our longing for union. It is divided into two main parts. First, the Pope develops an "adequate anthropology" based on the words of Christ. In order to have a "total vision of man," we must look to our experience of embodiment "in the beginning" *(Mt 19:8)*, in our history *(Mt 5:27-28)*, and in our destiny *(Mt 22:30)*. In the second part of his catechesis, John Paul applies his distinctive Christian humanism to the vocations of celibacy and marriage, and also to the moral issue raised by Pope Paul VI's encyclical *Humanae Vitae*.

Of course, in a brief chapter such as this, we can only provide a thumbnail sketch of the actual content of the Pope's revolutionary catechesis. We will begin with his main idea.

The Pope's Thesis

The Pope's thesis, if we let it sink in, is sure to revolutionize the way we understand the human body and sexuality. "The body, and it alone," John Paul says, "is capable of making visible what is invisible, the spiritual and divine. It was created to transfer into the visible reality of the world, the invisible mystery hidden in God from time immemorial, and thus to be a sign of it" *(Feb 20, 1980).*

A mouthful of scholarly verbiage, I know. What does it mean? As physical, bodily creatures we simply cannot see God. He is pure Spirit. But God wanted to make his mystery visible to us so he stamped it *into our bodies* by creating us as male and female in his own image *(Gn 1:27).*

The function of this image is to reflect the Trinity, "an inscrutable divine communion of [three] Persons" *(Nov 14, 1979).* Thus, in a dramatic development of Catholic thought, John Paul concludes that "man became the 'image and likeness' of God not only through his own humanity, but also through the communion of persons which man and woman form right from the beginning." And, the Pope adds, "On all of this, right from 'the beginning,' there descended the blessing of fertility linked with human procreation" *(ibid).*

The body has a "nuptial meaning" because it reveals man and woman's call to become a gift for one another, a gift fully realized in their "one flesh" union. The body also has a "generative meaning" that (God willing) brings a "third" into the world through their communion. In this way, marriage constitutes a "primordial sacrament" understood as a sign that truly communicates the mystery of God's Trinitarian life and love to husband and wife - and through them to their children, and through the family to the whole world.

Original Man

This is what Adam and Eve *experienced* "in the beginning." The very sentiment of sexual desire as God created it to be was to love as God loves in the sincere gift of self. Since this call to love is the summary of the Gospel, John Paul can say that if we live according to the nuptial meaning of our bodies, we "fulfill the very meaning of [our] being and existence" *(Jan 16, 1980)*. It is *for this reason* that a man clings to his wife and they become "one flesh" *(see Gn 2:24)*.

In his exegesis of the creation accounts, the Holy Father speaks of this *original unity* of the sexes as flowing out of the human being's experience of *original solitude*. Man realized in naming the animals that he *alone* was aware of himself and free to determine his own actions; he alone was *a person* called to love. It is on the basis of this solitude - an experience common to male and female - that man experiences erotic desire and his longing for union.

While among the animals there was no "helper fit for him," upon awaking from his "deep sleep" the man immediately declares: "This at last is bone of my bones and flesh of my flesh" *(Gn 2:23)*. That is to say,

"Finally, a *person* I can love." How did he know that she too was a person called to love? Her naked body revealed the mystery.

Prior to the rupture of body and soul caused by sin, the body enabled them to see and know each other "with all the peace of the interior gaze, which creates... the fullness of the intimacy of persons" *(Jan 2, 1980)*. Living in complete accord with the nuptial meaning of their bodies, the experience of original nakedness was untainted by shame *(Gn 2:25)*.

Historical Man

The entrance of shame indicates a radical change in their experience of embodiment. It indicates the loss of grace and holiness. "Original man" gives way to "historical man" who must now contend with lust in his heart.

Lust is erotic desire void of God's love. Hence, if we even look lustfully at others, we've already committed adultery in our hearts *(see Mt 5:28)*. Christ's words are severe in this regard. John Paul poses the question: "Are we to fear the severity of these words, or rather have confidence in their salvific content, in their power?" *(Oct 8, 1980)*.

Their power lies in the fact that the man who utters them is "the Lamb of God who takes away the sin of the world" *(Jn 1:29)*. Christ didn't die and rise from the dead merely to give us coping mechanisms for sin. His death and resurrection are efficacious. They effectively "liberate our liberty from the domination of concupiscence," as John Paul expresses it.

This means if we open our bodies once again to the "breath" of the Holy Spirit, we can experience a "real and deep victory" over lust. We can rediscover in what is erotic that original nuptial meaning of the body and live it. This liberation from lust is, in fact, "the condition of all life together in truth" *(Oct 8, 1980)*.

Eschatological Man

What about the experience of embodiment and our longing for union in the afterlife (eschaton) ? Didn't Christ say we will no longer be given in marriage at the resurrection *(see Mt 22:30)*? Yes, but this doesn't mean our longing for union (marriage) will be done away with. It means it will be *fulfilled*. Sacraments are merely earthly signs of heavenly realities. We no longer need signs to point us *to* heaven, when we are *in* heaven.

Heaven is the eternal consummation of the marriage between Christ and the Church. This is what we are created for. This is the ultimate longing of the human heart. And this is what the "one flesh" union points to from the beginning *(see Eph 5:31-32)*.

Hence, in the resurrection of the body we rediscover - in an eschatological dimension - the same nuptial meaning of the body in the meeting with the mystery of the living God face to face *(see Dec 9, 1981)*. "This will be a completely new experience," the Pope says, but "it will not be alienated in any way from what man took part in from 'the beginning,' nor from ...the procreative meaning of the body and of sex" *(Jan 13, 1982)*.

The Christian Vocations

Only by understanding *who man is* originally, historically, and eschatologically can we understand *how man is to live*. In other words, having outlined an "adequate anthropology," the door is now opened to a proper understanding of the Christian vocations of celibacy and marriage.

Those who are celibate "for the sake of the kingdom" *(Mt 19:12)* are choosing to live in the heavenly marriage on earth. In a way, they are "skipping" the sacrament to participate more directly in the *real thing*. By doing so, they step beyond the dimension of history - within the dimension of history - and declare to the world *that the kingdom of God is here (Mt 12:28)*. Authentic Christian celibacy, then, is not a rejection of sexuality or a devaluation of marriage. It is the expression on earth of its ultimate purpose and meaning.

As a vocation to holiness, marriage is meant to prepare men and women for heaven. But in order for it to be adequate heaven preparation, the model must accurately image the divine prototype. The sacramentality of marriage, then, consists in the manifesting of the eternal mystery of God in a "sign" that serves not only to proclaim that mystery, but also to accomplish it in the spouses *(see Sep 8, 1982)*.

All of married life constitutes this sign. But nowhere is this sign more dramatically manifested than when husband and wife become "one flesh." Just as the body expresses the soul of a person, the "one body" that spouses become in conjugal intercourse expresses the "soul" of their married life. "Indeed the very words 'I take you to be my wife - my husband,'" the Pope says, "can be fulfilled only by means of conjugal intercourse" *(Jan 5, 1983)*.

New Context for Sexual Morality

John Paul's original insights provide a whole new context for understanding the Church's teaching on sexuality, particularly her teaching against contraception. This is, in fact, the linchpin of all sexual morality. For as soon as sexual union is divorced from its inherent link with procreation, any means to sexual climax can be justified (the sexual revolution of the 20th century has certainly demonstrated this in practice).

Based on the logic of the theology of the body, one can speak of morality in the sexual relationship according to "whether or not it has the character of the truthful sign" *(Aug 27, 1980)*. All sexual morality, then, comes down to this simple question: Does this behaviour incarnate God's love or does it not?

For those who have been enlightened by the Holy Spirit to understand the "great mystery" of nuptial union, contraception is simply *unthinkable*. Nuptial union is meant to proclaim the mystery of the Trinity - that "God is life-giving love." In this sense the Pope says the "language of the body" is prophetic. However, an intentionally sterilized act of intercourse proclaims the opposite. It changes the "language of the body" into a specific *denial* of God's creative love, making the spouses "false prophets."

Nuptial union is also meant to be a sacramental sign of Christ's union with the Church. But for sacraments to convey spiritual realities, the physical must accurately symbolize the spiritual. Insert contraception into this picture and (knowingly or unknowingly) a couple engages in a *counter-sign* of Christ's union with the Church. This is why an intentionally sterilized act of intercourse can never consummate a marriage - it is a contradiction of the very essence of the "great mystery" of the sacrament.

Battle for the Meaning of Life

If, as John Paul teaches, the body *and it alone* is capable of communicating the mystery of God's love to us; and if there is an enemy of God who wants to keep us from God's love - where, then, would he go to do it? The Church Father Tertullian says that Satan attempts to counter God's plan of salvation by plagiarizing the sacraments. And where better to begin than with the "primordial sacrament"?

Satan's goal is to scramble the language of our bodies. And look how successful he has been. How many people, for example, think that the body and the gift of sexuality are the last places to look for the presence of God?

Much is at stake in our failure to understand the language of our bodies. As John Paul II says, this is obviously "important in regard to marriage." However, it "is equally essential and valid for the understanding of man in general" *(Dec 15, 1982)*. The theology of the body is, in fact, according to John Paul, the basis of the most suitable education in what it means to be a human being *(see Apr 8, 1981)*. Yes, the battle raging in our Church and our world regarding sexual morality is nothing short of a battle for the very meaning of human existence.

Hence, the theology of the body should not be considered merely a minor discipline among many in the overall scope of Catholic teaching. Again, according to the Holy Father, what we learn by reflecting on Christ's words in the theology of the body "is, in fact, the perspective of the whole Gospel, of the whole teaching, in fact, of the whole mission of Christ" *(Dec 3, 1980).*

In Conclusion

The theology of the body is a clarion call for the Church not to become more "spiritual," but to become more *incarnational.* It is a call to allow the Word of the Gospel to penetrate our flesh and bones. When this incarnation of the Gospel takes place in us, we see the Church's teaching on sexual morality not as an oppressive set of rules, but as the foundation of a liberating ethos, a call to experience the redemption of our bodies, a call to rediscover in what is erotic the original meaning of sexuality which is the very meaning of life. And this is the first step to take in renewing the world.

As John Paul asserts, man and woman's call to form a communion of persons "is the deepest substratum of human ethics and culture" *(Oct 22, 1980).* Thus, the dignity and balance of human life "depend at every moment of history and at every point of geographical longitude and latitude on 'who' she will be for him and he for her" *(Oct 8, 1980).* In short, a culture that does not respect the truth about sexuality is doomed to be a culture that does not respect the truth about life; it is doomed to be a culture of death.

This is why John Paul made the theology of the body the first catechetical project of his pontificate. At the heart of the new evangelization, at the heart of building a civilization of love and a culture of life, is marriage and the family. And at the heart of marriage and the family is the truth about the body and sexuality.

Let us live it and proclaim it. If we do, we will not fall short of renewing the face of the earth!

FAITH AND REASON IN THE TEACHING OF JOHN PAUL II

BY THOMAS G. WEINANDY, OFM, CAP.

Pope John Paul II, since his days as a young student, has always possessed a love for learning. He not only enthusiastically studied philosophy and theology, but also history and literature; and he even wrote his own poetry and plays. He taught for many years in the University of Krakow. John Paul perceived, it seems almost instinctively, the worth of the human person created in the image and likeness of God, and as such, the intellectual dignity and ability with which it was endowed. This dignity and ability can be stated simply: Human beings can know the *truth*.

The truth that human beings can know, so sharing in some small manner in the knowledge of God himself, is multifaceted. Human beings can not only know the truths of science, maths, and history, etc., but also the truth obtained through philosophy, primarily a knowledge about themselves and above all a knowledge of God. Within the Judeo-Christian tradition such knowledge could be obtained in a twofold manner.

Firstly, most of what human beings come to know is through the use of their naturally endowed intellect - the truths acquired through the use of reason alone. Secondly, the human intellect is so empowered that it is actually capable of receiving revelation from God, truth that, while beyond the scope of human reasoning, is not beyond the scope of human understanding. Human beings accept this truth of revelation in faith, that is, on the authority that it is revealed by God's word and action in their midst.

Calling man back to the Truth

Even before he became pope, John Paul detected that this awesome ability of human beings to know the truth, whether by reason or revelation, an ability that makes them truly human and so manifesting their likeness to God, had been for a long time not only undermined but even disparaged. Many held and were holding that human beings could not know the truth, and any attempt to obtain it was doomed to hopeless failure. It was from within this depressing intellectual climate that John Paul undertook to write, in 1998, his encyclical *Fides et Ratio (Faith and Reason)*. The present intellectual milieu 'has given rise to different forms of agnosticism and relativism which have led philosophical research to lose its way in the shifting sands of widespread scepticism' *(FR 5, see also 86-91)*. In the light of this scepticism the

Pope desperately wanted to call man back to the truth, to the truth of who he is, to the truth that he can know the truth, to the truth that comes by way of reason and to the truth that comes by way of faith.

John Paul begins his encyclical by stating:

"Faith and reason are like two wings on which the human spirit rises to the contemplation of truth; and God has placed in the human heart a desire to know the truth - in a word, to know himself - so that, by knowing and loving God, men and women may also come to the fullness of truth about themselves."

For John Paul, deep within the human heart there resides a longing to know the truth and the ultimate truth that human beings long to know is God himself. In so knowing God, human beings actually come to a knowledge of themselves, that is, they come to know that to be truly human is to live in communion with God. The Pope perceives that the whole of human history bears witness to this desire for the truth. Human beings persistently ask questions: Who am I? Where have I come from? Where am I going? Why is there evil? What is the meaning of life? *(see FR 1)*. The very act of questioning validates man's rationality (animals do not question) and in so doing validates man's ability to find answers to his questions - of finding the truth. Since the Church is on the same journey as the rest of humankind, John Paul holds that the Church has a special duty to serve humanity's quest for the truth by being a servant of the truth *(see FR 2)*. As a servant of the truth then John Paul professes and argues that this human desire for truth can indeed be obtained through faith and reason, particularly through philosophical reasoning.

The Truth of Faith

In the first chapter of *Fides et Ratio* John Paul sets out to establish the priority of revelation and the acceptance of that truth in faith. He states that the Church is 'the bearer of a message which has its origin in God himself. The knowledge which the Church offers to man has its origin not in any speculation of her own, however sublime, but in the word of God which she has received in faith' *(FR 7)*. In his love God has revealed himself not only so that humankind might have an objective knowledge of God, but also, within this knowledge, a full personal fellowship with him. This revelation is composed of God's deeds within our historical world and of words that make known the meaning and significance of these deeds.

"This plan of Revelation is realized by deeds and words having an inner unity: the deeds wrought by God in the history of salvation manifest and confirm the teaching and realities signified by the words, while the words proclaim the deeds and clarify the mystery contained in them. By this Revelation, then, the deepest truth about God and human salvation is made clear to us in Christ, who is the mediator and at the same time the fullness of all Revelation" *(FR 10)*.

While this truth that comes by way of revelation is not identical with nor exclusive of the truth that comes by way of philosophy, yet this knowledge is 'peculiar to faith' *(FR 8)*. According to John Paul, one believes so that one can know.

"Faith is of an order other than philosophical knowledge which depends on sense perception and experience and which advances by the light of the intellect alone. Philosophy and the sciences function within the order of natural reason; while faith, enlightened and guided by the Spirit, recognizes in the message of salvation the 'fullness of grace and truth' *(Jn 1:14)* which God has willed to reveal in history and definitively through his Son Jesus Christ" *(FR 9)*.

John Paul sees then that faith is primarily an act of obedience, an act of obedience to the authority of God who guarantees the truth of his own revelation. This act of faith for John Paul is of the utmost importance. 'Men and women can accomplish no more important act in their lives than the act of faith; it is here that freedom reaches the certainty of truth and chooses to live in that truth' *(FR 13)*. Thus the Pope concludes his opening chapter by declaring that

'Revelation is neither the product nor the consummation of an argument devised by human reason', yet
this revelation accepted by faith addresses the very
questions that human reason raises - the nature and
meaning of life *(FR 15)*.

"The ultimate purpose of personal existence, then,
is the theme of philosophy and theology alike. For all
their difference of method and content, both disci-
plines point to that "path of life" *(Ps 16:11)* which, as
faith tells us, leads in the end to the full and lasting
joy of the contemplation of the Triune God" *(FR 15)*.

The Relationship Between Faith and Reason

John Paul continues to articulate the significance of
this relationship between faith and reason. This relationship is seen within the Old Testament Wisdom
literature. There faith awakens reason to see what it
may have been blind to without the light of faith.
'Faith', the Pope states, 'liberates reason to attain
correctly what it seeks to know' *(FR 20)*. The Book
of Wisdom proclaims that humankind can come to a
knowledge of God by contemplating his works of
creation (see *Ws 13:5* and also *Rom 1:20*). The
whole cosmic order is a '"a book of nature", which
when read with the proper tools of human reason,
can lead to knowledge of the Creator" *(FR 19)*. If
human beings fail to recognize God in his creation it

is not due to some lack in their ability, but rather their freedom and sin impede them.

John Paul notes that, from its earliest days, the Church has engaged itself with philosophical thinking *(see Acts 17:18)*. The Fathers of the Church entered into dialogue with the philosophical currents of their day and often used philosophical concepts to help clarify and defend the Gospel mysteries. For the Pope the same dialogue is even more necessary today. He emphasizes that, while reason cannot pass judgement on the content of faith, for it is incapable of doing so, yet it 'can find meaning, to discover explanations which might allow everyone to come to a certain understanding of the contents of faith' *(FR 42)*. Thus reasoned argument can lead to and foster faith. Not only does one believe so as to understand, but one can also understand so as to believe. Moreover, reason is an indispensable tool for obtaining a deeper understanding of the faith. As both St. Augustine and St. Anselm emphasized: 'Faith seeks understanding'. Therefore, the Pope again expresses a common theme within the encyclical: The contents of faith need the help of reason in order to be more fully understood and reason finds its goal in the contents of faith.

"The fundamental harmony between the knowledge of faith and the knowledge of philosophy is once again confirmed. Faith asks that its object be understood with the help of reason; and at the summit of its searching reason acknowledges that it cannot do without what faith presents" *(FR 42)*.

Thus, faith has nothing to fear from reason, but actually seeks it out and trusts in it. John Paul laments that sometimes in the past a distrust of reason has led to 'fideism', that is, the stance that faith has no communality with reason but stands alone and even in opposition to reason *(see FR 55)*.

Reclaiming the Dignity of Reason

However, today the crucial issue that confronts humankind is that reason wishes to separate itself from faith, and in so doing actually has lost confidence in its own ability to know the truth. Much of contemporary philosophy not only refuses to undertake the grand crusade to know the truth, but also holds that such a crusade cannot be undertaken. This, the Pope declares, leads to Nihilism, the claim that nothing can be known to be absolutely and irrevocably true *(see FR 45-48)*. Moreover, such philosophical scepticism undermines the truth of faith. If no truth can be known, then the truth of faith cannot be known. Likewise, the Pope insists that while the Church does not embrace or canonize any particular philosophy, yet the Church must defend the content of faith from being subsumed within some philosophical system. This reduces revelation to mere philosophical insights obtained by reason alone and disallows the distinctive and non-reducible revelation that comes from God alone *(see FR 49-53)*. It must be remembered, insists John Paul, that revelation as expressed within Sacred Scripture and the Church doctrinal tradition contain within them certain philosophical presuppositions which cannot be violated without doing violence to God's revelation *(see FR 55)*. By this the Pope means that to disallow, on philosophical grounds, the supernatural intervention of God such as professed in the Incarnation, the resurrection, miracles and sacramental actions, would be philosophically erroneous. In this light the Pope boldly declares 'that faith and philosophy recover the profound unity which allows them to stand in harmony with their nature without compromising their mutual autonomy. The *parrhesia* [outspokeness] of faith must be matched by the boldness of reason' *(FR 48)*.

While the Pope desires to protect the truth of the Christian faith against a misuse of reason and philosophy, he is most concerned, in the encyclical, to foster a proper use of reason and encourage humankind, particularly philosophers, not to abandon reason but to recognize the dignity and power that resides within reason.

"In the light of faith which finds in Jesus Christ this ultimate meaning, I cannot but encourage philosophers - be they Christian or not - to trust in the power of human reason and not set themselves goals that are too modest in their philosophizing. The lesson of history in this millennium now drawing to a close shows that this is the path to follow: it is necessary not to abandon the passion for ultimate truth, the eagerness to search for it or the audacity to forge new paths in the search. It is faith which stirs reason to move beyond all isolation and willingly to run risks so that it may attain whatever is beautiful, good and true. Faith thus becomes the convinced and convincing advocate of reason" *(FR 56)*.

The irony is that John Paul believes that modern men and women have lost their 'faith' in reason because they have lost their faith in God's revelation. Conversion to the Gospel then becomes the means by which one not only obtains salvation, but, in so doing, one also recaptures one's human dignity. To believe in divine revelation, far from being in irrational act inimical to reason, actually becomes the act by which human beings regain confidence in their own rationality. For the Pope, then, faith does not undermine the integrity of reason; rather faith sustains reason and provides reason the confidence to search for and grasp the truth even in areas that reason, left to itself, would never consider. On the one hand, through the truths of faith 'reason is offered guidance and is warned against paths which would lead it to stray from revealed Truth and to stray in the end from the truth pure and simple'. On the other hand, faith stirs reason 'to explore paths which of itself it would not even have suspected it could take ... reason discovers new and unsuspected horizons' *(FR 73, see also 74-9)*. The Pope ardently calls, therefore, for philosophy to undertake its proper tasks with confidence, specifically the study of metaphysics, that is, that philosophical study which goes beyond the merely scientifically empirical and addresses the very nature of being. This includes the study of the universal principles within the created order, the nature and freedom of man, the manner in which humans come to know truth, and the discerning of what is truly good and beautiful *(see FR 75-86)*.

Philosophy and Theology

One of the central concerns within *Fides et Ratio* is that of the relationship between philosophy and theology, for here reason and faith are necessarily most intimately and inseparably entwined. John Paul first makes a very crucial distinction. He distinguishes the *auditus fidei*, that is, the hearing of the proclaimed faith, and the *intellectus fidei*, that is, the intellectual understanding of the faith *(see FR 65)*. The content for the study of theology, for the *intellectus fidei*, is the *auditus fidei*, that is, the revealed truths proclaimed in the Bible and the Church's doctrinal tradition and taught authoritatively by the Magisterium. Theology is not the source or arbiter of what is to be believed. The theologian must accept in faith, as do all Christians, what has been revealed by God and proclaimed by the Church. To undertake the task of Christian theology without holding in faith what has been proclaimed by the Church is not to do Christian theology at all, but merely to engage in philosophical speculation which will ultimately lead to heresy.

Nonetheless, theology does undertake the noble and essential task of using reason to aid the Church's understanding of what is believed in a number of ways, for, again, faith itself, under the impulse of the Holy Spirit, seeks to understand more deeply what is believed. Firstly, theology contributes to a proper understanding of what is to be believed in faith. Thus, for example, theology can help explain what it means for the one God to be a Trinity of persons so as to help the non-believer come to faith and the believer to grasp more clearly what is believed. Secondly, theology can employ words and concepts that foster a greater depth of understanding of what is believed. For example, the Church always believed that Jesus was truly God and truly man, but through the aid of theology the Church has come to express this faith by stating that Jesus is the one *person* of the Son of God existing in two *natures*, as God and as man. The concepts of 'person' and 'nature' deepen and clarify the mystery of the Incarnation. Thirdly, theology fosters a clearer understanding of the salvific meaning of the various doctrines and their interrelationship. For example, theology can help the Church better understand the salvific meaning of the Incarnation and its relationship with the Resurrection and Pentecost, or its relationship with Baptism and the Eucharist. In the performance of these various tasks John Paul holds that the theologian must always utilize the sacred and authoritative sources of Scripture and the Church's tradition. Moreover, the theologian employs reason and philosophy, guided and protected by these sacred sources, to grasp more fully and explain more clearly the marvellous salvific mysteries contained within these sacred sources *(see FR 66-73)*.

Conclusion

We find then in Pope John Paul's encyclical, *Fides et Ratio*, not merely a proclamation and defence of the truth of the Christian and Catholic faith, but more so a summons to the more fundamental truth that human beings can know the truth. Truth can be known either by faith or by reason, and together they promote the proper dignity and validity of each. In conclusion the Pope turns to Mary, as *Seat of Wisdom*. As Mary did not lose her authentic humanity in accepting God's word spoken to her 'so too when philosophy heeds the summons of the Gospel's truth its autonomy is in no way impaired. Indeed, it is then that philosophy sees all its enquiries rise to their highest expression' *(FR 108)*. For John Paul, to reason and to know the truth is to be in the image of God, and to employ one's intellect in the service of the Gospel is to become truly human.

THE ECUMENICAL TEACHING OF JOHN PAUL II

BY DAVID CARTER

Pope John Paul II has consistently reiterated both the Catholic Church's commitment to the cause of Christian Unity and his own very personal commitment to it. A desire to foster true ecumenism has been a key motive for many of his visits, especially those to Constantinople in 1979, to Germany in 1980, to Britain in 1982, to the Scandinavian countries in 1993 *(TMA 24)* and more recently to Greece in May 2001. The Holy Father has welcomed countless representatives of other churches to Rome and given innumerable homilies and addresses on ecumenical topics. He has devoted two major encyclicals to ecumenism, *Orientale Lumen* (*Light from the East*) of 1994 and *Ut Unum Sint* (*That They May All Be One*) of 1995. He also gave special prominence to ecumenism in his apostolic letters in preparation for and in celebration of the millennium, *Tertio Millennio Adveniente* (*As the Third Millenium Approaches*) of 1994 and *Novo Millennio Ineunte* (*At the Beginning of the New Millenium*) of 2001.

Rooted in Vatican II

The Pope's teaching is rooted solidly in that of the Second Vatican Council which he quotes repeatedly. He refers to its "enormously rich body of teaching" and its "striking new tone", so relevant to the times *(TMA 20)*. He calls on Catholics to examine their consciences as to how far they have internalised its teaching. Particularly, he asks whether the Church "leaves room for charisms, ministries and different forms of participation by the people of God" *(TMA 36)*. This links with his repeated teaching that ecumenism is an integral part of Christian living, in which everyone, according to their capacity and opportunities, should be involved. Ecumenism is not a "sort of appendix" to the Church's normal life; rather, it is "an organic part of her life and work, and consequently must pervade all that she does" *(UUS 20)*.

The Pope emphasises the fullness of the Father's gracious plan as the final context of ecumenism. "God wills the Church because He wills unity and unity is an expression of his agape (love)" *(UUS 9)*. He stresses that disunity is a counter-witness, marring the missionary effectiveness of the Church. It must be overcome if the world is to believe the Gospel.

The Holy Father's teaching balances the need for human activity in repentance and conversion with the indispensable role of the Holy Spirit, as he said in

Canterbury in 1982 "who alone can lead us" on the path to unity. All Christians must experience a conversion, a real change of mind, where unity is concerned. He said early in 2000: "The longing for unity goes hand in hand with a profound ability to sacrifice whatever is personal, in order to dispose the soul to ever greater fidelity to the Gospel. Preparing ourselves for the sacrifice of unity means changing our viewpoint, broadening our horizons, knowing how to recognise the action of the Holy Spirit who is at work in our brethren, discovering new dimensions of holiness and opening ourselves to fresh aspects of Christian commitment".

Historical Perspective

Christians must repent of their own and renounce the past sins of their spiritual ancestors against unity. The Pope has himself taken the lead in this process, for example, by apologising, on a recent visit to the Czech republic, for the intolerance and violence perpetrated by past Catholics against Protestants in that country. He calls on all to realise that the truth "cannot impose itself except by virtue of its own power"(*TMA 35*). He also calls for the purification and reconciliation of memories. This last point has become an important aspect of ecumenical conversation, involving the re-reading of the history of the tragic divisions of the past impartially, with each side recognising where it was at fault rather than trying to saddle the other side with all the blame, while exonerating itself.

The Pope stresses the enlargement of spiritual vision that can come about through true ecumenism. "Thanks to ecumenism, our contemplation of the 'mighty works of God' has been enriched by new horizons... [and] the knowledge that the Spirit is at work in other Christian communities"*(UUS 15).*

Importance of Shared Prayer

Prayer is also at the heart of the ecumenical movement, not just prayer for other Christians but especially *shared* prayer with them. "Fellowship in prayer leads people to look at the Church and Christianity in a new way" *(UUS 23).* It is from self-denial and new attitudes that the spirit of unity can grow. We see here a parallel with the thinking of the Methodist ecumenical pioneer, William James Shrewsbury (1785-1866), who commended to the Methodist people the virtue of "disinterestedness". By that he meant an attitude that delighted in truth and holiness wherever encountered and in whatever church.

At the same time, the Holy Father emphasises that unity cannot come by human effort alone. It is the work of the Holy Spirit. He alone can lead us. It is His gift *(Canterbury address, 1982; TMA 34).*

Our preparation involves his action in us. "Preparing ourselves..means changing our viewpoint, broadening our horizons, knowing how to *recognise the action of the Holy Spirit*, opening ourselves to fresh aspects of Christian commitment". It is above all the Spirit who removes the barriers to our appreciation of other churches by opening our eyes to His "work in other Christian communities" *(UUS 15)*. One matter that should be explained is the Pope's distinction between "churches" and "ecclesial (or Christian) communities" in his writing. He confines the use of the term "church" primarily to those Orthodox and Oriental churches which have, in Roman Catholic eyes, preserved the valid episcopate and full sacramental structure necessary for full recognition as "particular" and local "churches". The term "ecclesial communities" is used of those reformation and post-reformation churches that, according to current Catholic teaching, lack such an episcopate and structure.

Not a compromise

The Pope also balances very carefully the claims of truth and love. He is insistent that unity cannot come about by fudge or compromise. In theological dialogue, the churches must be loyal to the truth. Sitting light to the truth can only result in what the Pope, following the Council, calls "false irenicism", that is a false attempt to conciliate.

The Pope is very clear about where remaining difficulties lie in ecumenical conversation. He recognises that for Orthodox and reformation churches alike, his own ministry is a particular stumbling block. In the case of the reformation and post-reformation churches, he singles out five questions as particularly difficult and needing great patience and care. The first is the relationship between 'sacred Scripture, as the highest authority in matters of faith, and Sacred Tradition, as indispensable to the interpretation of the Word of God". The second is the eucharist, the third the sacramental nature of ordination. The fourth is the nature of the magisterium or teaching office of the Church. Lastly, he mentions the understanding of the Virgin Mary "as Mother of God and icon of the Church" *(UUS 79)*.

Despite all these grave difficulties, the Pope gladly recognises, and is greatly personally encouraged by, the elements of truth that exist in all the churches. He particularly stresses that they have all produced their saints and martyrs. He asserts that "perhaps the most convincing form of ecumenism is the ecumenism of the saints and martyrs... the *communio sanctorum* (the communion of saints) speaks louder than the things that divide us" *(TMA 37, cf UUS 1)*. He calls for the

Church to be diligent in keeping the roll of the martyrs and in treasuring their memory. He acknowledges
that martyrs have come alike from the Catholic,
Orthodox, Anglican and Protestant churches *(UUS
84)*. One may here add that many non-Catholics hope
that soon it may be possible for all to accept a common martyrology and venerate, in common, the memory of all who have provenly given their lives in witness to Christ.

Exchanging Gifts

Loyalty to the truth, and honesty in the face of difficulties, do not mean that, in dialogue, the churches
might not advance together towards new and *fuller*
appreciations of the truth than they have previously
received in separation. In *Orientale Lumen*, the Pope
particularly emphasises that the different ways in
which the ancient eastern churches have lived and
thought about the faith are not necessarily contradictory to those lived and cherished in the Latin West. At
certain points, the insights of East and West enrich
each other, enabling the Church, as he puts it, "to
breathe with both its lungs".

The Pope places great emphasis upon theological
dialogue. He stresses that this is not just a matter of
interchange of ideas and theological insights but "an
exchange of gifts", of spiritualities developed and

lived in the power of the Spirit *(UUS 28)*. In a particularly interesting passage in *Ut Unum Sint*, he talks of the way in which the Church has been enriched during the years of separation by the development of differing styles of spirituality and service within the separated churches. "In spite of fragmentation, which is an evil from which we need to be healed, there has resulted a kind of rich bestowal of grace which is meant to embellish the *koinonia*" *(UUS 85)*.

The Pope sets dialogue within the widest possible context as something integral to human nature as God intended it to be. "Dialogue is an indispensable step along the path towards human self-realisation, the self-realisation both of each individual and of every human community" *(UUS 28)*. Implicit in his statement is the belief that every Christian community, whether or not the Roman Catholic Church can recognise it as "fully" church, has gifts to offer, perhaps "unexpected ones" *(UUS 15)*. The Pope endorses the widespread emerging consensus throughout the mainstream Christian churches that there is a legitimate and enriching diversity of styles in which the Christian life can be lived and Christian truth expressed. In several notable cases he has hailed and endorsed key advances in the recognition of this. With certain of the ancient "Oriental Orthodox" churches Catholics have reached agreement that certain varying ways concerning the relationship

between Christ's divine and human natures are no
longer to be seen as contradictory and church dividing,
but, rather, as complementary and enriching, contribut-
ing to a profounder appreciation of the mystery of
Christ as true God and true man. Most recently, the
Pope has also endorsed the *"Common Statement on
Justification"* also accepted both by the Lutheran
World Federation and the Catholic Church. While this
does not solve all the problems on the way to
Lutheran-Catholic reconciliation, it has removed the
oldest subject of dispute between them. The Pope has
also asserted that the consensus statement, with its
careful juxtaposition of Catholic and Lutheran
"emphases" "must come to influence the life and
teachings of our churches". Perhaps it was particularly
in anticipation of this final agreement that the Pope
made his statement in 1995 that "dialogue makes possible surprising discoveries" *(UUS 38).*

Reuniting East and West

Two aspects of the work for unity, the Pope has particularly made his own. The first is the quest for re-union
with the Orthodox. As a Pole, a member of a slav
nation, the Pope is well aware that the majority of his
fellow slavs are Orthodox. At the beginning of his pontificate, he even dared to express the hope that East and
West might be reunited in time for the millennium. He

is particularly concerned to end the ill-feeling that for so long prevailed between eastern rite Catholics in communion with Rome (represented primarily in England by the Ukrainian diocese) and Orthodox. He is also anxious to remind Latin rite Catholics of the equal dignity of the ancient eastern traditions of theology and spiritual life that are shared both by Orthodox and eastern rite catholics. This he did in the encyclical, *Orientale Lumen*. He drew attention to the eastern tradition of holiness of *"theosis"* or growth in holiness by sharing in the energies of the Holy Trinity. He also commended the eastern tradition of seeing monasticism not as a model for a spiritual elite, but as setting a standard of self-discipline for all Christians.

In his encyclical, *Ut Unum Sint*, he acknowledged the problems other Christians have in accepting his focal ministry of unity as Bishop of Rome. He pointed to his own weakness and constant need of God's forgiveness, stressing that Peter had only received his charge after revealing his weakness and being rehabilitated by the Lord. He then applied the principle of free dialogue to his own office. Noting that the Catholic Church could never renounce the "Petrine" ministry, with which it believes it has been entrusted for the sake of ensuring the unity of all, he nevertheless offered to discuss with the leaders and theologians of other churches how his ministry might be exercised in

a manner they could find more acceptable. He accepted that he needed the advice of others in order to find
better ways of serving the unity of all God's people.
"This is an immense task..which I cannot carry out by
myself. Could not the real, but imperfect communion
existing between us persuade church leaders and their
theologians to engage with me in a patient and fraternal dialogue on this subject..in which..we could listen
to one another, keeping only before us the will of
Christ for his Church?" *(UUS 96)*.

Partial Communion

Particularly significant is the emphasis which the
Pope places upon the "partial communion" already
exiting between Catholics and all the other churches.
Since Vatican II the key development in the understanding of the Church in all the major Christian traditions has been a profound re-reception of the concept
of the Church as communion, as a constant partnership between pastors, people and those with special
charisms or insights. This was a point made in the
recent Catholic-Methodist dialogue report, *"The Word
of Life"* when it spoke of the continuing "fruitfulness
of faith" in developing styles of spirituality and service. It was in this context that the Pope in his most
recent unity week sermon urged all Christians to
"appreciate more fully what we already share.

Important elements of holiness and truth, which belong to the one Church of Christ, even outside the visible boundaries of the Christian Church urge us on to full unity". He constantly urges the *practice* of communion. In *Orientale Lumen*, he cited Paul's longing to visit the Roman church that "our faith might be mutually strengthened" *(Rom 1:12, OL 45)*. He calls for the ecclesiology of communion, adumbrated in the conciliar decree *Lumen Gentium*, to be strengthened *(TMA 36)*. He says, "to make the Church the home and school of communion: that is the great challenge facing us in the new millennium that is beginning" *(NMI 43)*.

Conclusions

To conclude with a couple of observations; firstly, that the Holy Father maintains a sane balance between hope and recognition of the many difficulties on the ecumenical path. In 2000 he said, "The ecumenical journey is certainly still difficult, and will perhaps be long, but we are encouraged by the hope that comes from being led by the presence of the Risen One and the power of his Spirit, always capable of new surprises" *(NMI 12)*.

Secondly, writing as a Methodist ecumenist and studying the contributions of John Paul II, it is striking just how much his basic teaching on ecumenical method tallies with the Methodist view and, indeed, that of other non-Catholic churches. These would agree with him that much needs still to be studied and resolved, especially, though not exclusively, on the five points he referred to in *Ut Unum Sint* (para 79). His spiritual approach and emphases upon the Holy Spirit, on holiness and on the understanding of the Church as communion are heartily concurred with. His willingness to discuss the exercise of his ministry of unity a potential service to us all, his emphasis upon legitimate and enriching diversity and his stress upon the possibility of surprising discoveries are all welcomed. It may indeed be fitting to conclude with a quotation from the ecumenical spiritual tradition of the Methodist Conference which resonates so much with the Pope's teaching. In 1820, the Wesleyan Methodist Conference reminded the Methodist people that they were "the friends of all and the enemies of none" and that "towards all denominations of Christians they should ever maintain the kind and catholic spirit of primitive Methodism". This statement breathes and advocates the same spirit of love that is present throughout the ecumenical writing of the present Pope.

JOHN PAUL II REACHES OUT - INTERRELIGIOUS DIALOGUE

By ✠ MICHAEL L. FITZGERALD

Karol Wojtila was elected pope on 16 October 1978, choosing the name John Paul II as a sign of continuity. In April of the following year he received in audience the members and consultors of the Secretariat for Non Christians (which he was later to rename Pontifical Council for Interreligious Dialogue). He said to them:

"The late Paul VI, who founded this Secretariat, and so much of whose love, interest and inspiration was lavished on non-Christians, is no longer visibly among us, and I am convinced that some of you wondered whether the new Pope would devote similar care and attention to the world of the non-Christian religions."

Answering his own question, John Paul II referred to his first encyclical, *Redemptor Hominis*, published the previous month, in which he had remarked how the Second Vatican Council had given "a view of the terrestrial globe as a map of various religions". He spoke of the esteem the Council had shown for the values enshrined in other religions, and concluded with a firm assurance: "The non-Christian world is indeed constantly before the eyes of the Church and of the Pope. We are truly committed to serve it generously".

Together for an end to conflict

John Paul II has most certainly lived up to this commitment. He did not hesitate to accept the invitation of the King of Morocco, Hassan II, to address young Muslims. Some 80,000 listened to him in the stadium of Casablanca in August 1985. In January of the following year, in New Delhi, he visited the monument to Mahatma Gandhi. For long moments he knelt down in silent prayer and then rose to speak in praise of the "apostle of non-violence". On 13 April 1986 the Pope made a historic visit to the Rome synagogue. On 27 October of the same year he welcomed in Assisi religious leaders, both Christians and people of other religions, whom he had invited to come together to pray for peace in the world. This day was important both for its contents and its style. The religious leaders gathered around the Pope in friendship, united in fasting and also in the final fraternal meal. Prayers were offered, but care was taken that distinctions of belief not be blurred. The Pope himself drew a lesson from the events of the day, saying:

"Let us see in it an anticipation of what God would like the developing history of humanity to be: a fraternal journey in which we accompany one another toward the transcendent goal which he sets for us."

This Day of Prayer in Assisi, seen by so many thanks to television, truly caught the imagination and aroused in people of different religions a desire to meet. In many parts of the world, in Kyoto, Japan, in Montreal, Canada, in Westminster, London, in Washington D.C., similar gatherings have been held. During the Gulf War, in numerous places, Jews, Christians and Muslims felt the need to pray together for an end to the conflict. As people become conscious of the growing religious plurality of today's world, so the necessity is recognised of engaging in relations which cross religious boundaries.

A Christ-centred dialogue

In his teaching ministry the Pope has reflected on the impact of religious plurality. He sees it as his mission to apply the vision of the Second Vatican Council. So time and again he returns to the teaching of *Nostra Aetate*, the Declaration on the relations of the Church to Non Christian religions. Speaking once to Bishops from Iran he stated:

"The Second Vatican Council's declaration *Nostra Aetate* gives clear indications that inspire the Church for its interreligious dialogue. They are mainly: respect for one's personal conscience, rejecting all forms of coercion or discrimination with regard to faith, freedom to practice one's religion and give witness to it, as well as appreciation and esteem for all genuine religious traditions."

For John Paul II the vision of the Council is centred on Christ. Already in his first encyclical, *Redemptor Hominis*, he had emphasised a line from the document on the Church in the Modern World: "For, by his incarnation, he, the Son of God, has in a certain way united himself with each man" (*Gaudium et Spes* 22). He often refers to this truth in order to show that the Church, and therefore also the Pope, must be interested in all human beings, and not be deterred by religious differences. Similarly he returns to another affirmation found in the same paragraph of *Gaudium et Spes*:

"Since Christ died for all *(Romans 8:32)*, and since all men are in fact called to one end and the same destiny, which is divine, we must hold that the Holy Spirit offers to all the possibility of being made partners, in a way known to God, in the paschal mystery *(GS 22)*."

So people are not to be condemned just because they are not Christians. Recognizing that God, through the Holy Spirit, is at work in them, it is possible to engage in a dialogue which is not mere politeness but is a form of entering into the paschal mystery, a death to egoism in order to live for others. This is truly a dialogue of salvation.

A dialogue led by the Spirit

It should not be thought that this emphasis on dialogue signals an end to the missionary outreach of the Church. Vatican II's decree on the missionary activity of the Church, *Ad Gentes*, states clearly that "the pilgrim Church is missionary by her very nature" *(AG 2)*. John Paul II, in order to stimulate the faithful application of the Council, has written an important missionary encyclical, *Redemptoris Missio*. It should be noticed that this letter adopts a broad understanding of what mission is. It is not confined to the explicit proclamation of the name of Jesus Christ, but comprises other activities of the Church, including interreligious dialogue. It states very clearly: "Interreligious dialogue is a part of the Church's evangelizing mission". It explains further:

"Dialogue does not originate from tactical concerns or self-interest, but is an activity with its own guiding principles, requirements and dignity. It is demanded by the deep respect for everything that has been brought about in human beings by the Spirit who blows where he wills."

Two elements in this passage are worth noting. The first is the intrinsic value of interreligious dialogue. It is not to be considered as a mere preparation for the task of proclamation or announcing Jesus Christ and inviting people to become members of the Church through baptism. It has its own aim which is to enable people of different religions to live in harmony and peace, to understand one another better, to work together on behalf of humanity, and to help one another to respond to God's call. Dialogue and proclamation are not to be opposed. Dialogue itself contains an element of proclamation insofar as it includes witness to one's own beliefs, while proclamation can never be an imposition of the truth but must always be conducted in a spirit of dialogue. They are both activities of the Church; to be carried out in obedience to the promptings of the Holy Spirit.

This leads to the second observation, the importance of the Spirit. The Spirit was already mentioned in the quotation given above from *Redemptoris Missio*. The passage continues:

"Through dialogue, the Church seeks to uncover the 'seeds of the Word' *(AG 11,15)*, a 'ray of that truth which enlightens all men' *(NA 2)*; these are found in individuals and in the religious traditions of mankind. Dialogue is based on hope and love, and will bear fruit in the Spirit. Other religions constitute a positive challenge for the Church; they stimulate her both to discover and acknowledge the signs of Christ's presence and the working of the Spirit, as well as to examine more deeply her own identity and to bear witness to the fullness of Revelation which she has received for the good of all."

In a previous section of the encyclical, building on an earlier teaching which he had given in *Dominum et Vivificantem*, a letter explicitly dedicated to the Holy Spirit, John Paul II had referred to the universal action of the Spirit, affecting "not only individuals but also society and history, peoples, cultures and religions". It was this trust in the work of the Spirit, he said, that had guided him in his meetings with a wide variety of people. So he was led to reaffirm a conviction he had expressed on the occasion of the Assisi Day of Prayer for peace: "Every authentic prayer is prompted by the Holy Spirit, who is mysteriously present in every human heart".

In the light of Vatican II

For John Paul II the Second Vatican Council was a providential preparation for the Third Millennium. In his letter *Tertio Millennio Adveniente*, inviting the Church to prepare for the Great Jubilee which was to usher in this millennium, he reflected on the Church's rediscovery of her own identity and on the call to conversion and renewal which this entailed. "On the basis of this profound renewal, he stated, the Council opened itself to Christians of other denominations, to the followers of other religions, and to all the people of our time". In preparation for the Jubilee the Pope invited the Church to engage in a three-year reflection, concentrating each year on a Person of the Blessed Trinity. The final year was dedicated to the Father. The Pope suggested that this would be an appropriate time to reflect on the unity of the human family, despite all the divisions that exist within it, including those of a religious nature. He therefore encouraged interreligious dialogue, stating:

"In this dialogue the Jews and the Muslims ought to have a preeminent place. God grant that, as a confirmation of these intentions, it may also be possible to hold joint meetings in places of significance for the great monotheistic religions. In this regard attention is being given to finding ways to arrange historic meetings in places of exceptional symbolic importance - like Bethlehem, Jerusalem and Mount Sinai - as a means of furthering dialogue with Jews and the followers of Islam, and to arrange similar meetings elsewhere with the leaders of the great world religions."

The Holy Father was able, at least partially, to fulfil his desire to make his own Jubilee pilgrimage to places of significance in the history of salvation. Though

because of the circumstances he was unable to undertake the Abrahamic lap of the journey, which would
have taken him to Ur in Southern Iraq (a special commemoration of Abraham in the Vatican, at which some
Jews and Muslims were present, replaced this leg of
the pilgrimage), he did manage to follow in the steps
of Moses in Egypt and to accomplish his own pilgrimage to the Holy Land. There was no interreligious
gathering on Mount Sinai, as had been hoped, but the
Pope had a very significant and remarkably cordial
meeting with Muslim leaders at al-Azhar, in Cairo. In
Jerusalem a meeting of Jews, Christians and Muslims
did take place, though not without some tension aris-
ing over diverse claims to the Holy City. The Holy
Father also had separate meetings with both Jewish
and Muslim religious leaders.

A call to unity of the whole human family

A call had been made for a more general gathering of
people of different religions. Accordingly, in October
1999, just before the opening of the Great Jubilee, the
Pontifical Council for Interreligious Dialogue organ-
ised an Interreligious Assembly, *On the eve of the
third millennium, collaboration between different
religions*. Some 200 persons, about half Christians
and half people of other religions, were invited to
participate. The meeting was held within the Vatican,

though on the third day the participants went together to Assisi, on the actual anniversary of the historic Day of Prayer for Peace. On the fourth and final day, a message formulated by the participants was proclaimed in St Peter's Square, during a ceremony attended by thousands and presided over by John Paul II. The Pope took the occasion to reiterate his own convictions regarding intereligious dialogue. His words may form a fitting conclusion to this reflection on his teaching on this matter.

"I have always believed that religious leaders have a vital role to play in nurturing that hope of justice and peace without which there will be no future worthy of humanity. As the world marks the close of one millennium and the opening of another, it is right that we take time to look back, in order to take stock of the present situation and move forward together in hope towards the future...

As we survey the situation of humanity, is it too much to speak of *a crisis of civilization* ? We see great technological advances, but these are not always accompanied by great spiritual and moral progress. We see as well a growing gap between rich and poor... Then there are the many conflicts continually breaking out around the world...

Surely this is not the way humanity is supposed to live. Is it not therefore right to say that there is indeed a

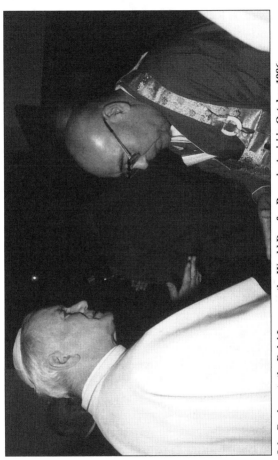

John Paul meets the Dalai Lama on the World Day for Peace in Assisi in October 1986.

crisis of civilization which can be countered only by *a new civilization of love*, founded on the universal values of peace, solidarity, justice and liberty *(TMA 52)* ?

There are some who claim that religion is part of the problem, blocking humanity's way to true peace and prosperity. As religious people, it is our duty to demonstrate that this is not the case. Any use of religion to support violence is an abuse of religion...

The task before us is therefore *to promote a culture of dialogue*. Individually and together, we must show how religious belief inspires peace, encourages solidarity, promotes justice and upholds liberty...

Our hope rises not merely from the capacities of the human heart and mind, but has a divine dimension which it is right to recognize. Those of us who are Christians believe that this hope is a gift of the Holy Spirit, who calls us to widen our horizons, to look beyond our personal needs and the needs of our particular communities, to the unity of the whole human family...

Our gathering here today in St Peter's Square is another step on that journey. In all the many languages of prayer, let us ask the Spirit of God to enlighten us, guide us and give us strength so that, as men and women who take their inspiration from their religious beliefs, we may work together to build the future of humanity in harmony, justice, peace and love."

The Church in Eastern Europe: Martyrdom and Ecumenism

By Neville Kyrke-Smith

There are two strands of papal thinking which can be drawn out of all the Pope's heartfelt writings and speeches on Eastern Europe: martyrdom and ecumenism. From his own Polish background - amidst the suffering of the peoples of Central and Eastern Europe - Pope John Paul II has developed what is almost a new spirituality, focussing on the Cross as the key to hope and unity for Europe and the world.

The keys of faith, hope and charity - the Keys of St Peter - helped open a door between East and West when the Iron Curtain fell and the Berlin Wall came down. The message of the Holy Father in recent times is that *'the path we must now walk'* together - in charity and truth - is to unify and strengthen the witness of Christ to the world. For as he said in *Novo Millennio Ineunte*:

"Unhappily, as we cross the threshold of the new millennium, we take with us the sad heritage of the past... there is still a long way to go. (But) it is on

Jesus' prayer and not on our own strength that we base the hope that even within history we shall be able to reach full and visible communion with all Christians... May the memory of the time when the Church breathed with 'both lungs' spur Christians of East and West to walk together in unity of faith and with respect for legitimate diversity, accepting and sustaining each other as members of the one body of Christ" *(NMI 48)*.

Yet, it is in the *'ecumenism of holiness'* to which the Pope refers (as in his address in Greece to the Holy Synod, 4 May 2001), and the witness of the martyrs, which underpin this real desire for unity. Thus martyrdom and ecumenism are intimately linked in the mind and heart of this pontiff from the borders of Eastern Europe.

Martyrdom

For one amazing papal event of the Great Jubilee Year 2000 was not fully understood. On 7 May 2000, simple candle lamps were lit in front of Rome's ancient Colosseum at the Ecumenical Commemoration of Witnesses to the Faith in the 20th century - a period of suffering and martyrdom with more martyrs than any previous century. The 'witnesses' of the last one hundred years who suffered for their faith included a large number from the East amongst the 12,000 listed by

Rome. The names included both martyrs and also those who endured hardship and persecution for their loyalty to Christ. As I watched those lamps glow in that damp, grey evening, the significance of the celebration became apparent. There was something radical and truly uniting as testimonies from every continent and representing all vocations were read out. The Pope in gold cope and mitre, in the centre of this gathering, was surrounded by senior clergy from other ecclesial bodies; the candles were lit and prayers were offered as incense was burned. The historical setting called to mind the witness of the early martyrs. Forget *Gladiator* the film - this was about the Torch of Faith, which has been passed on to us!

In the *Papal Bull of Indiction of the Great Jubilee of the Year 2000*, the Holy Father stated: "A sign of the truth of Christian love, ageless but powerful today, is the memory of the martyrs. Their witness must not be forgotten. They are the ones who have proclaimed the Gospel by giving their lives for love. The martyr, especially in our own days, is a sign of that greater love which sums up all other values. The martyr's life reflects the extraordinary words uttered by Christ on the Cross: 'Father, forgive them, for they know not what they do'" *(Luke 23:34)* (13).

Staying faithful to the Gospel

And for two and a half hours at the Colosseum testimonies were given - as the Holy Father said - of the "countless numbers [who] refused to yield to the false gods of the twentieth century" and of those who "had rejected a way of thinking foreign to the Gospel of Christ." Significantly, the first such witness selected was the Patriarch Tichon of the Russian Orthodox Church, who wrote in 1918 that "the Lord has raised up a series of new martyrs who have had a share in his Passion, bishops and priests... killed and tortured by crazed and unhappy children of our country." The second testimony came from Ol'ga Jafa, witness of the Solovki Islands, where behind five-metre-thick monastery walls religious prisoners were entombed in one of the most infamous gulag camps. She had described how, in this detention centre and death camp for hundreds of religious, "united in their labours, a young Catholic bishop and an old Orthodox bishop worked together... carrying their load... who shared in the same undertaking, a union in love and humility."

Other testimonies chosen from the 12,000 witnesses were powerfully portrayed. The Romanian Greek Catholic Bishop Joan Suciu, who died in prison in 1953, wrote that "Good Friday has arrived for the Church." The words of the remarkable Father Anton Luli, the Albanian Jesuit who was imprisoned or serving hard

labour for twenty-eight years, described the crucifix-
ions and the appalling tortures endured in prison:
"many of my confreres died as martyrs: it was my lot,
however, to remain alive in order to bear witness."
Other powerful testimonies were read out by representatives from around the world. Then finally the words
of the late Supreme Catholicos of all Armenians, His
Holiness Karekin I, who died in 1999: "Yes!
Suffering, persecutions, destruction, massacres, depor-
tation, genocide...and what else! We have committed
many errors in the past; but we have not committed the
error of losing faith and hope. That has been, to my
understanding, the secret of our survival."

Passing on the Torch of Faith

The Pope prayed that "from the witnesses of faith...
may the younger generation receive the torch of faith,
in order to bear witness to the Risen Christ." The
torches - the lamps - burned in front of the
Colosseum. The blood of the martyrs and this witness
of faithful Christians called for unity, forgiveness and
faith. At the Regina Caeli on the 7 May, the Holy
Father said that in the shadow of the Cross the ecumenical differences pale into insignificance: "The
courage they demonstrated in taking up the Cross of
Christ calls out to us with a voice louder than any fac-
tors of division."

Perhaps we were seeing the outcome of that remarkable encyclical *Fides et Ratio* (published on the Feast of the Triumph of the Cross), in which the Holy Father wrote: "the martyrs... are the most authentic witnesses to the truth about existence. The martyrs know that they have found the truth about life in the encounter with Jesus Christ, and nothing and no one can take this certainty from them." He continues, "This is why to this day the witness of the martyrs continues to arouse such interest, to draw agreement, to win such a hearing and to invite emulation... Their words inspire confidence [...] as the truth we have sought for so long. [They] provide evidence of love, and stir in us a profound trust [...] : they declare what we would like to have the strength to express." *(FR chapter 3, 32)*

Christ. The Cross. The martyrs. Truth. Love. Reconciliation. I suppose we should not be surprised that Pope John Paul II was, in the evening of his life, holding a torch of faith and redeeming love to the world. This great Jubilee celebration may not have caught the imagination of the world in the way that his visit to the Holy Land did, or the Jubilee appeal for forgiveness for past wrongs. Yet a torch of faith has been held aloft, for as the Pope said: "The new generations must know the price of the faith they inherit, so they may take up with gratitude the torch of the Gospel and illuminate with it the new century and the new millennium."

The divisions between the Churches do not reach up to heaven

We can also recall how the sufferings of the gulag prison camps brought an ecumenism of the heart: as when the Lithuanian Catholic priest (now Archbishop) Sigitas Tamkevicius and the Russian Orthodox priest Gleb Yakunin worked together in Perm 36. Not long ago, the bodies of Catholic priests were discovered alongside those of Russian Orthodox priests and bishops, just north of St Petersburg - proof that, as Fr. Alexander Men (an Orthodox priest who was murdered in 1990) once said, "the divisions between the Churches do not reach up to heaven." The blood of the martyrs of the camps intermingled.

Whilst it is not just in the East that we can speak of genocide and martyrs, the history of the Soviet gulag prison camps where between 20 and 30 million died has not been fully recognised; there has not been the chance to identify the perpetrators, the complicity of others, or even to recognise the need for reconciliation. Now the Russian government has stated that at least 200,000 Orthodox priests and religious died in Russia during the 1930's under Stalin - many crucified to the doors of their churches - and the Russian

Orthodox have three books detailing their martyrs of the 20th century. But this is only a beginning. Perhaps the Holy Father, by looking East, is reminding us of the central message of the Gospel - the death and resurrection of Love: for in the light of the Cross the Church offers hope despite the worst endeavours of man. This is implied by those words attributed to the Pope: "*Lux ex Oriente* - Light from the East": the torch of faith shining from the martyrs' witness reflecting their faith in the Resurrection of Christ.

Unity

It is from the Cross that the reconciling words of Christ echo across the world, "Father, forgive them for they know not what they do," *(Luke 23:34)*. It was also just before His Passion that Jesus prayed: "That they may all be one," *(John 17:21)* and these words are now described by Pope John Paul as a *'command'* (Letter to Metropolitan Volodymyr of Kyiv, 26 March 2001). Christ's words from the Cross encapsulate the call for unity: "It is on Jesus' prayer and not on our own strength that we base the hope that even within history we shall be able to reach full and visible communion with all Christians" *(NMI 48)*.

Yet the reality of ecumenical tensions, accusations of proselytism and the burden of history have recently been evident in Ukraine, concerning the visit of the

Holy Father in June 2001. In this border land - on the fault line between East and West - 'the three Romes' seemed to be trying for poll position in the race to get there first: the Ecumenical Patriarch Bartholomew of Constantinople, Patriarch Alexei of Moscow and Pope John Paul II. Yet the view and perspective of the present Pope has always been that the unity of the Church is vital for a true witness to Christ: the Church 'must breathe again with both lungs'. Perhaps, as Cardinal Lubomyr Husar asked and prayed, Ukraine may yet become a bridge and not a barrier: "Please help us regenerate Ukraine. We can be a bridge between East and West, but there has to be two-way traffic. Despite everything we have the gift of hope. So perhaps the Latin-Rite Church can also learn something from us - an Eastern tradition in a Catholic edition." The challenge of Ukraine is a challenge at the heart of the Gospel both the West and the East: reconciliation and unity.

A united witness to Christ

The call for unity is a call for a united, true and powerful witness to Christ, as the Holy Father wrote to Metropolitan Volodymyr of Kyiv (after the Russian Orthodox Metropolitan of Kyiv and All Ukraine had written in March 2001 objecting to the Pope's planned June 2001 visit to Ukraine): "My forthcoming visit... is also meant to express a constant and respectful attention to our Orthodox brethren, along with a firm commitment to continue on the way of dialogue in truth and charity." As well as hoping that the Mixed Commission of Churches would begin working as soon as possible, the Pope wrote that of his desire and "longing for unity, following the Divine Master's command *ut unum sint*, 'that they all may be one'" and his wish to show with "a fraternal embrace my love for you and for all the faithful of the Ukrainian Orthodox Church." He concluded: "Until then, may the Lord grant us an awareness of the longing we share for the unity of all Christians. It is indispensable, if the proclamation of the Gospel is to resound with new fervour throughout the world, until the time when the day comes, awaited by all, of the joyful encounter with the Risen Christ."

At the *ad limina* visit of the Catholic bishops and Apostolic administrators of Russia, the Caucasus and Central Asia on 9 February 2001, the Pope said: "Although the difficulties of daily life are inevitable, you can overcome them with the Lord's help by following the dialogue of charity. This is how individual gifts serve the good of the entire Body of Christ. Respectful dialogue also becomes a patient methodology, making it possible to establish relations with other baptised faithful living in Russia. Seek whatever fosters mutual understanding and, when possible, co-operation: this is a concrete rule of ecumenical dialogue that was so dear to Blessed John XXIII, who loved to say again and again that what unites us is much greater that what divides us. This is why we should not be discouraged by the difficulties and even the failures of the ecumenical journey, but sustained by prayer, we must continue making every effort to establish full unity among Christ's disciples. With trust in God, with charity, with constancy we can help to hasten the divine Master's ardent desire 'that they may all be one... so that the world may believe'" *(John 17:21)*. Archbishop Tadeusz Kondrusiewicz replied to the Pope that "Despite persecution and suffering, the Church in Russia survived. She has become a Church of martyrs, whose witness will never be forgotten."

A dialogue of truth and a dialogue of charity

The Pope is calling for both *'a dialogue of truth'* and *'a dialogue of charity'*. In all of his writing and words he recognises the great needs in Eastern Europe and how the divisions within the Church compound the problems and undermine the Gospel of faith, hope and charity. Faith is needed: for it is the people and the laity whose faith suffers as a result of church property disputes in Romania, Ukraine and elsewhere. Charity is needed: to help - for example - the millions who resort to abortions every year in Ukraine, Russia and the other countries of the Former Soviet Union - and a united Church could bring more effective charitable help and teach the Gospel of Life. Hope must be offered: for the social problems are immense as in Yakutsk, in north-eastern Siberia, where over 50 per cent of the men are alcoholics, children are fleeing appalling domestic violence and the Salesians who run a youth mission for over 150 children and the Orthodox in their parishes could offer more hope to the people if they worked together.

There are some positive signs of co-operation and the beginnings of an ecumenical path. In many ways the fall of communism, and the corrupt capitalism and machinations of the mafias of present-day Russia, have shown how far the people have fallen: but as some of the sects realised - there is an opportunity to present Christ as a real hope for both individuals and society as a whole. One project in particular has caught the imagination of Catholics in the West: Aid to the Church in Need has supported two Orthodox chapel boats, with a third under construction, on the Volga and Don rivers. These boats visit villages and towns where there is no church or where the churches were destroyed. The priest and deacon engage in primary evangelisation with the priest baptising, blessing and celebrating the Liturgy for people who have not been able to learn about God for over 70 years. Snippets of good news cannot be exaggerated, but somehow it is these local and diocesan spiritual links which can be built into bridges of trust. An Orthodox abbot emphasised that this is the most important aspect of aid to the Orthodox, telling me "this initiative comes at a vital time... because it is so important for us and our faith."

The Vision

"How good and how pleasant it is, when brothers live in unity!" (Ps. 133:1).

Our Lady stood at the foot of the Cross. The icon on the wall of the papal apartments at St Peter's, the icon of Our Lady of Kazan and the bullet from the assassination attempt on his life now in the statue of Our Lady of Fatima, all illustrate the great devotion of Pope John Paul for the Mother of God. It is through Our Lady's prayers - as well as those of the martyrs - that he trusts unity in truth and charity can be found. The devotion in the East to Our Lady can unite us under her protecting veil amidst the storms of modern life. For Pope John Paul said in Athens *(4th May 2001)*:

"The Virgin Mary, by her prayer and maternal presence, accompanied the life and mission of the first Christian community gathered around the Apostles *(cf. Acts 1:14)*. With them she received the Spirit at

Pentecost! May she watch over the path that we must now walk in order to move towards full unity with our brethren of the East and in order to fulfil with one another, in openness and enthusiasm, the mission that Christ has entrusted to His Church. May the Virgin Mary - so venerated in your country... lead us always to her Son Jesus" *(cf. John 2:5)*.

So - although accusations, misunderstandings and distrust still abound - the Pope is calling for a united witness to Christ. He knows the problems and challenges, as seen at the Emmitsburg meeting of the Joint International Commission for Theological Dialogue between the Catholic and Orthodox Churches in August 2000, or in the talk of a 'cold war' between the Churches by Metroplitan Kirill in February 2001. Yet Pope John Paul is emphatic that disunity is a real scandal and a stumbling block to the mission of the Church and primary evangelisation. It is as he turns us to the centre of our faith, the Cross, that he can say that "by fixing our gaze on Christ the Great Jubilee has given us a more vivid sense of the Church as a mystery of unity" *(NMI 48)*.

There is real hope in the Pope's vision that in the shadow of the Cross ecumenical differences can pale into the shade. At the ecumenical celebrations of St Stephen of Hungary in August 2000, it was the first time a saint recognised by the West was also recognised by

Orthodox Churches since the schism of 1054. In Syria, a shared church is being built for Catholic (Melkite) and Orthodox Christians sponsored partly by Aid to the Church in Need in Dummar, a suburb of Damascus. As well as the chapel boats these are the beginning of a fulfilment of the vision and desire for unity.

The Holy Father called (in 1995) for charitable gestures of love, calling it "an imperative of charity" (*Ut Unum Sint*) to help our brothers and sisters in Christ in Russia. The Pope wrote in his Apostolic Letter *Orientale Lumen (OL 23)*: "To extend gestures of common charity to one another and jointly to those in need will appear as an act with immediate impact. The Lord's call is to work in every way to ensure that all believers in Christ will witness together."

The Pope appreciates the depths and beauty of the Eastern traditions, recognising how the Faith is taught in the liturgy. It is one of his great desires to see both Catholics and Orthodox move towards unity at the beginning of this Millennium. He has even invited discussion on how his role of Pope may evolve. His desire for unity and co-operation with the Orthodox was clearly stated when he encouraged Catholic Patriarchs to help restore full unity with Orthodox Churches, at a meeting in September 1998, quoting *Orientale Lumen (OL 1)*, "that the full manifestation of the Church's catholicity (may) be restored to the

Church and to the world, expressed not by a single tradition, and still less by one community in opposition to the other ... God's entire Word must be heard, for the words of the West need the words of the East, so that God's Word may ever more clearly reveal its unfathomable riches."

As he wrote early in 2001: "In the perspective of our renewed post-Jubilee pilgrimage, I look with great hope to the Eastern Churches, and I pray for a full return to that exchange of gifts which enriched the Church of the first millennium. [...] Theological discussion on essential points of faith and Christian morality, co-operation in works of charity, and above all the great ecumenism of holiness will not fail, with God's help, to bring results. In the meantime we confidently continue our pilgrimage, longing for the time when, together with each and every one of Christ's followers, we shall be able to join wholeheartedly in singing: 'How good and how pleasant it is, when brothers live in unity!'" *(Ps. 133:1; NMI 48).*

In the spirit of the Great Jubilee the Pope continues to reflect on the great harm done by the schism of 1054 and the sack of Constantinople in 1204 and recognizes that "past and present controversies and... enduring misunderstandings" mean we now need the "liberating process of the purification of memory". It is in the light of the Second Vatican Council's call on

Catholics to regard the members of other Churches "as brothers and sisters in the Lord" (*Unitatis redintegratio 3*) that he calls anew for unity and his dramatic apology in Greece reflects this *(Address to Holy Synod, 4 May 2001)*: "For all the occasions past and present, when sons and daughters of the Catholic Church have sinned by action or omission against their Orthodox brothers and sisters, may the Lord grant us the forgiveness we beg of him."

It may not prove possible for this particular Polish Pope to meet this Patriarch, but let us look over the horizon - in faith, hope and charity. The witness and prayers of the martyrs lead us to the Cross, where stands Our Lady looking up at her son: the prayer of Christ from the Cross pleads for forgiveness and reconciliation - "Father forgive them for they know not what they do" *(Luke 23:34)*. It is this Pontiff who is trying to build a bridge with the Cross so that the Gospel can be proclaimed more powerfully in both East and West.

'TOTALLY YOURS'–THE TEACHING OF JOHN PAUL II ON OUR LADY

BY JOHN SAWARD

Every Papal motto conveys a theological message. When a new Pope chooses a phrase to sum up the aspirations of his pontificate, he makes a statement that he wants the whole Church on earth to hear. The motto of the present Holy Father is 'Totally Yours' (*totus tuus*). He addresses the words to our Lady, who is symbolized by the letter 'M' under the cross on his coat of arms. By this heraldic device, John Paul II in 1978 declared his desire to belong totally to Mary, so that he could belong totally to Jesus. He saw, and he wanted the whole People of God to see, that no one is better placed than the Mother to help us know and love the Son: through Mary, the Holy Spirit leads us to Jesus, and so to the Father. The Pope borrowed the words 'Totally Yours' from St Louis-Marie de Montfort, who, in the Jansenist-blighted France of the early eighteenth century, reminded Catholics that the surest and straightest road to union with the Divine Saviour is devotion to the Blessed Virgin. That is the truth John

Paul learnt from Louis-Marie, and that is the truth he wants to get across to all of Christ's faithful.

When he writes or speaks about the Mother of God or indeed any other sacred subject, the Pope does not propagate some private theology of his own. The Vicar of Christ receives authority from God to strengthen his brethren in the universal and unchanging faith of the Church *(cf. Lk 22: 32)*, the faith once delivered to the saints *(Jude 1:3)*. He has the power to exercise his teaching office in an extraordinary way, *ex cathedra*, by defining a doctrine as a dogma of the faith, that is, as a truth that God has revealed, and that the children of the Church must accept with the assent of faith. However, up to now he has not deployed this most weighty instrument of papal magisterium. Instead, he has strengthened the faith of his brethren by ordinary means - by encyclicals, letters, and constitutions, and by an abundance of addresses and homilies delivered either in Rome or on his many travels abroad. In all of these documents, the Pope applies his personal talents - as poet, dramatist, and philosopher - to his official task as the Teacher of All Christians. In its content, his teaching about our Lady is in perfect continuity with that of his predecessors; only in its quantity, style, and emphases does it stand out as different. The quantity is certainly great. On 25 March 1987, at the beginning of the Marian Year, the Pope published an encyclical on the 'Mother of the Redeemer' (*Redemptoris Mater*). He has made our Lady the subject of a long series of catechetical addresses, and on her feast-days and at her shrines throughout the world, he has preached countless homilies in her honour. In fact, you will find the holy name of Mary, Virgin and Mother, in almost every document promulgated by the Pope. He believes, as the Fathers of the Second Vatican Council proclaimed, that the Mother of God sheds light on all the doctrines of the faith and on every question that engages the heart of man *(see LG 65)*. A poet's appreciation of beauty moves him to praise the Mother of Fairest Love a phrase used in his *Letter to Families (see LF 20 and LA 16)*. A dramatist's sense of the struggle of good and evil helps him perceive the ways in which the Mother of the Redeemer brings the grace of her Son into the history of nations and the lives of individuals *(RM 52)*. His dedication to the truth, as a philosopher, disposes him to see the Seat of Eternal Wisdom as 'a sure haven for all those who devote their lives to the search for wisdom' *(FR 108)*.

Since the Holy Father's task is to expound the Church's teaching concerning our Lady, the best way to approach his Mariology is to consider what he has to say about the four dogmas defined by the Church through Councils and Popes: our Lady's *Divine*

Motherhood, Perpetual Virginity, Immaculate Conception, and Assumption. In addition, we need to turn our own minds to the mystery that has particularly absorbed his own: our Lady's *Co-operation with the Work of Redemption*, both on earth in the obscurity of faith and in Heaven in the light of glory. This is a revealed doctrine that comes down to us from the Apostles through the ordinary, day-to-day teaching of the Pope and the bishops in communion with him.

The Divine Motherhood of Our Lady

The name 'Mother of God' (*Theotokos* in Greek) is the greatest of our Lady's titles, and the reality of being the Mother of God is the reason for all of her other privileges. Like the Fathers of the Church before him, the Pope argues that when we call the Blessed Virgin 'Mother of God', we sum up everything the Church believes about her Son, who is true God and true man in one person:

"Mary is the Mother of God (*Theotokos*), since by the operation of the Holy Spirit she conceived in her virginal womb and gave to the world Jesus Christ, the Son of God, of one substance with the Father. Thus, through the mystery of Christ, on the horizon of the Church's faith, there shines the mystery of His Mother. The dogma of Mary's divine motherhood was for the Council of Ephesus, and is for the

Church, like a confirmation of the dogma of the
Incarnation, in which the Word truly assumes human
nature into the unity of His person without cancelling
out that nature" *(RM 4)*.

The Church's doctrine about our Lady
('Mariology') is an essential part of her doctrine
about our Lord ('Christology'). You cannot have
orthodox faith in Jesus as God-made-man unless you
acknowledge Mary as the Mother of God. By the
same token, the man who would be orthodox will
never separate Mary from Jesus and His Church. To
make this point, the Pope adapts one of his favourite
texts from the documents of the Second Vatican
Council. We can only understand the mystery of
man in the light of the God-Man, and only in that
same light can we understand the mystery of Mary
(RM 4 cf. GS 22).

The dogma of our Lady's divine motherhood has
many moral applications. By making Mary to be His
Mother, God has raised up all womanhood to a
grandeur beyond compare. Our Lady, says the Pope,
is 'the new beginning of the dignity and vocation of
women, of each and every woman' *(MD 3)*. Her
humble *Yes* to God, her transparent openness to His
will and action, reveals femininity's most beautiful
face *(MD 11)*. The greatest exaltation of human
nature took place in the male sex, when the divine

person of the Word became man and male, the New Adam. But the greatest exaltation of the human person took place in the female sex, in the New Eve, in whose flesh and by whose faith the Word became man and male. If Jesus is God, and Mary is His Mother, then every human being, man or woman, has a literally divine motive for honouring women and respecting what the Pope calls the uniquely 'feminine genius' *(MD 31 and LW 11)*. The greatest after God is a woman.

The Perpetual Virginity of Our Lady

Every privilege that God bestows upon Mary, whatever she by His grace says or does, is for the sake of Jesus and His Church. It is therefore for Him that she is 'Ever Virgin'. It is because of who her Son is, the eternally begotten Son of the Father, true from true God, that by the overshadowing of the Holy Spirit she conceives Him without seed and gives birth to Him without corruption. And it is in His honour that she consecrates her whole self, in body and in soul, to remain a virgin forever. The virginity of our Lady is, therefore, as the Holy Father says, 'a Christological theme before being a Mariological theme'. Like the wood of the Cross or the wrappings in the Empty Tomb, it is a 'reason and sign for recognizing in Jesus of Nazareth the Son of God'.

In his great charter for the family, *Familiaris consortio*, the Holy Father shows how Christian virginity and marriage support and explain each other. They are the two God-given ways in which the human person, as a unity of body and soul, can fulfil the vocation to self-giving love *(FC 11)*. In Mary these two vocations coincide in the most beautiful way. From her earliest days, out of a bridal love for God, she resolves to live for ever as a virgin ('I know not man', *Lk 1:34*), and out of that same love, in obedience to her divine Spouse, she agrees to be betrothed to Joseph *(cf. Lk 1:27)*. What is more, her consent to divine motherhood also springs from 'her total self-giving to God in virginity'.

"Mary accepted her election as Mother of the Son of God, guided by spousal love, the love that totally consecrates a human being to God. By virtue of this love, Mary wished to be always and in all things 'given to God', living in virginity. The words 'Behold the handmaid of the Lord' show that from the outset she accepted and understood her motherhood as a total gift of self, a gift of her person to the service of the saving plans of the Most High" *(RM 39)*.

Our Lady becomes the Mother of God, not despite her virginity, but in and through it. The centre of her maidenhood is also the heart of her motherhood: an unreserved *Yes*, the total gift of herself, in faith and love, to the Triune God.

The Immaculate Conception of Our Lady

Our blessed Lord is the cause of our Lady's Immaculate Conception. He is its 'principal efficient cause': it is God the Son who, with God the Father and God the Holy Spirit, fills the Blessed Virgin with sanctifying grace from the very beginning of her existence. He is also the purpose, the 'final cause': Mary is conceived immaculate, so that she can be a 'worthy dwelling place' (cf. the Collect for the Solemnity of the Immaculate Conception) for the Father's only-begotten Son. And Christ our Saviour also provides the 'meritorious cause': it is by the merits of His Passion, working backwards in time, that the soul of His Mother is preserved from all stain of Original Sin in the very instant of her conception. Jesus redeems us by setting us free from the Original Sin that we inherit from Adam at our conception, but He redeemed His Blessed Mother by preserving her from ever contracting Original Sin. So powerful is the Precious Blood of the Saviour that it can even reach back into history to touch the beginning of His Mother's existence: 'in the event of the Immaculate Conception the Church sees projected and anticipated, in her most noble member, the saving grace of Easter' *(RM 1)*.

The key, then, to the Christ-centredness of our Lady is the mystery celebrated on the eighth of December:

"Because of the richness of the grace of the beloved Son, by reason of the redemptive merits of the One who willed to become her Son, Mary was preserved from the inheritance of Original Sin. *From the first moment of her conception - that is to say, of her existence - she belonged to Christ.* From then on, she partook of saving and sanctifying grace, and of that love which has its beginning in the 'Beloved', the Father's Son, who through the Incarnation became her own Son" *(RM 10)*.

'No one in the history of the world', says the Holy Father, 'has been more Christ-centred' than Mary. Her whole mission is to bring Jesus to men and men to Jesus. For this our Lord predestined and created her, and for this He filled her with His grace from her conception. Mary is centred on Christ by Christ. That is why true devotion to her is the best way for us, too, to live a truly Christ-centred life in faith, hope, and charity. By her example and intercession, she enables us to say with St Paul: 'it is no longer I who live but Christ who lives in me, and the life I now live in the flesh I live by faith in the Son of God, who loved me and gave Himself for me' *(Gal 2:20; see also RH 22)*.

The Assumption of Our Lady

From the earliest years of his pontificate, Pope John Paul II has reminded us that our final hope is for the 'redemption of our bodies' *(cf. Rom 8:23)* in the general resurrection on the last day. 'Redemption', he says, 'is the way to the resurrection.' The Son of God did not cast off His human body when He ascended into Heaven. It was in the flesh that He ascended into Heaven, and in the flesh He will come again from Heaven on the last day. Then He will make the righteous share His risen splendour in the totality of their human nature: 'our commonwealth is in heaven, and from it we await a Saviour, the Lord Jesus Christ, who will change our lowly body to be like His glorious body, by the power which enables Him even to subject all things to Himself.' *(Phil 3:20f)*

The Blessed Virgin is united to the Divine Redeemer in an altogether unique way, and so her share in the effects of His redeeming work is also correspondingly unique. Our Lord did not wait to glorify her body till the day of His Second Coming; no, He took her into heavenly glory, in both body and soul, 'when the course of her earthly life had been completed'. The whole person of our Lady is already radiant with the risen beauty of her Son. Thus, according to the Holy Father, our Lady's Assumption is 'a providential stimulus to meditate on the exalted dignity of every human being, *including his bodily aspect*'. And the dogmatic meditation is accompanied by a moral exhortation: the glorification of our Lady's body urges us to present our own bodies 'as a living sacrifice, holy and acceptable to God.' *(Rom 12:1)*

When he defined the dogma of the Assumption, Pope Pius XII left open the question of our Lady's death. He was content to assert, in the words just quoted, that the Mother of God was assumed, body and soul, 'when the course of her earthly life had been completed'. Now, according to most of the Church's Doctors, many liturgical texts of East and West, and the dominant tradition of Christian iconography, our Lady did indeed suffer the separation of soul and body at the end of her earthly life. If this is so, then her Assumption was her anticipated resurrection, the re-uniting of her soul and body in glory. However, a small number of theologians have argued in recent centuries that our Lady was glorified in body and soul without suffering death; she therefore enjoyed a special gift of bodily immortality. In 1997, as part of his catechesis on our Lady, Pope John Paul gave this subject the most detailed consideration it has ever received from a Pope. Without making it a matter of *ex cathedra* definition, the Holy Father stated unambiguously that our blessed Lady did die at the end of her earthly life:

"True, Revelation presents death as a punishment for sin. Still, the fact that the Church proclaims Mary to be free from Original Sin by a singular divine privilege does not force the conclusion that she also received bodily immortality. The Mother is not superior to the Son, who assumed death, giving it a new meaning and transforming it into an instrument of salvation." *(General audience address 25 June 1997)*

Death comes to us a consequence of Original Sin, but death comes to Mary Immaculate as a consequence of human nature. Human nature is mortal, unless God somehow makes it immortal, but the Tradition does not compel us to conclude that God extended this privilege to His Blessed Mother. On the contrary, it would seem that He wanted her to experience human suffering and death, as He did, 'in view of the redemption of mankind'. The Holy Father expresses his agreement with St Francis de Sales, who said that the Blessed Virgin passed away through an ecstasy of love for her Son: she was transported out of this life 'in love, because of love, and through love' *(25 June 1997)*. The death of our Lady, which the Tradition prefers to call her 'Dormition' or 'Falling Asleep', is full of consolation for us mortal men. Mary, who out of love for Jesus suffered death and, by Jesus' love for her, has received the gift of resurrection, draws close with her motherly compassion to every dying person. 'By sharing the common lot of men, she can more effectively exercise her spiritual motherhood towards those who have reached the final hour of their lives' *(25 June 1997)*.

Our Lady's Co-operation with the Redemption

God does not just use the Blessed Virgin, in a passive way, to supply the matter from which His Son's human body was formed. He gives her the grace to co-operate with Him in a conscious and free way *(cf. LG 56)*. Yes, the womb that bore Christ and the paps that gave Him suck are greatly blessed, but blessed still more are the immaculate mind and heart that embraced Him in loving faith and obedience *(cf. Lk 11:27)*. *'Blessed is she who believed ... (Lk 2:45)*. These words of St Elizabeth at the time of the Visitation lie at the centre of the Holy Father's encyclical on our Lady. In her believing, the Mother of the Redeemer goes before every one of Christ's faithful. *(cf. RM 28,30, & 49)* She is the first and most perfect embodiment of Catholic faith *(cf. RM 13)*. That is why we can say that, before a single Apostle has been called, Holy Church exists in Holy Mary. And what she began by her faith at the Annunciation she continued throughout the hidden life and public ministry of her Son until at last, on Calvary, she was united with Him in His dereliction and experienced, as the Pope says, 'the deepest *"kenosis"* (emptying) of faith in human history' *(RM 18)*. On Calvary, through the unique privilege of her divine motherhood, our Lady co-operated with the redeeming work of her Son - what theologians call the 'objective redemption' - in an altogether unique way. In the words of the Second Vatican Council, to which the Pope constantly refers:

"The Blessed Virgin went forward in her pilgrimage, and faithfully persevered in her union with her Son even unto the Cross. There she stood, in keeping with God's plan, enduring with her only-begotten Son the intensity of His suffering. She associated herself with His sacrifice in her maternal heart, and lovingly consented to the immolation of this Victim that was born from her" *(LG 58)*.

Our Lady gives her consent to the sacrifice of her Son. She not only shares the intensity of His Passion but also, by faith and charity, identifies herself with the intentions of that Passion, namely, atonement for the sins of mankind. In this way, the Mother of God makes her contribution to the salvation of mankind. As the Holy Father says in his letter on human suffering, the sorrows of Mary became 'supernaturally fruitful for the redemption of the world. Her ascent of Calvary and her standing at the foot of the Cross, together with the Beloved Disciple, were a special sort of sharing in the redeeming death of her Son' *(Salvifici Doloris 25)*.

Once, by her loving faith, our Lady co-operated with her Son's redeeming work on earth, with His meriting for us of the divine life of grace. Now, by her loving intercession, she co-operates with the pouring out of redeeming grace from Heaven - what Catholic theologians call the 'subjective redemption'. Through this co-operation with the divine Mediator, our Lady can be called 'Mediatrix'. As the Holy Father says, citing the words of *Lumen gentium*:

"Mary, 'by her maternal charity, cares for the brethren of her Son who still journey on earth surrounded by dangers and difficulties, until they are led to their happy homeland'. In this way, Mary's motherhood continues unceasingly in the Church as the mediation which intercedes, and the Church expresses her faith in this truth by invoking Mary 'under the titles of Advocate, Auxiliatrix, Adjutrix, and Mediatrix'" *(RM 40, citing LG 62).*

When the Pope and his predecessors use titles like 'Mediatrix' to speak of our Lady, they are not placing her on the same level as her Son. How could they? He is Almighty God; she is but His creature - the greatest of His creatures, yet still only a creature, made by Him out of nothing and only raised up to her wondrous offices and privileges by His election and grace. The exalted titles of our Lady speak not of competition and rivalry but of a co-operation and participation made possible by God's condescending love. If Christ's members share in His Sonship by grace, as sons-in-the-Son, it should not surprise us if He makes His Mother share His mediation as a Mediatrix-in-the-

Mediator. This great principle of Catholic dogma - the principle of participation in Christ - was set forth with great clarity by the Fathers of the Second Vatican Council, and is re-stated by Pope John Paul in *Redemptoris Mater*:

"No creature could ever be classed with the Incarnate Word and Redeemer. However, just as the priesthood of Christ is shared in different ways both by sacred ministers and by His faithful, and as the one goodness of God is in reality communicated diversely to His creatures, so also the unique mediation of the Redeemer does not exclude but rather gives rise among creatures to a manifold co-operation, which is but a sharing in this unique source" *(LG 62; cf. RM 38)*.

Like everything else that is Christian, the mediation of our Lady is great because it is humble. It is a 'subordinate role', a service performed by the Handmaid of the Lord in utter dependence upon His own mediation: 'Mary entered, in a way that was all her own, into the one mediation "between God and men" which is the mediation of the man Christ Jesus' *(RM 39)*. Our Lady's mediating mission 'flows from the superabundance of Christ's merits, is founded on His mediation, absolutely depends upon it, and draws all its efficacy from it' *(LG 60; cf. RM 38)*. What is 'special and extraordinary' *(cf. RM 38)* about Mary's mediation points to what is special and extraordinary about her: it is the work of the incomparably great and humble Mother of God, who is more closely united to her Son than any other created person, and therefore draws more abundantly upon His grace. If we want to understand it more completely, we should meditate on the wedding at Cana, for there, as now in Heaven, our Lady interceded with our Lord on behalf of human need:

"She puts herself 'in the middle', that is to say she acts as a Mediatrix not as an outsider, but in her position as mother. She knows that as such she can point out to her Son the needs of mankind, and in fact, she 'has the right' to do so. Her mediation is thus in the nature of intercession: Mary 'intercedes' for mankind. And that is not all. As a mother she also wants the Messianic power of her Son to be manifested, that saving power of His which is meant to help man in his misfortunes, to free him from the evil which in various forms and degrees weighs heavily upon his life" *(RM 21)*.

When our Lady mediates grace by her prayers, she serves our Lord as His handmaid and helps us as our Mother. The mediation of Mary is, as the Pope says, a '*motherly* mediation' carried out by the Woman whom the crucified God-Man made the Mother of all His disciples *(cf Jn 19: 26f)*. Both on earth and in Heaven, the motherly heart of Mary reaches out to those for whom Jesus suffers and dies. By her co-operation with His work of restoring the supernatural life of grace to souls, she is 'a mother to us in the order of grace' *(cf. LG 61; RM 22, 38ff)*. She first exercised that motherhood on earth by consenting to the meriting of grace, and now in Heaven, 'until the final fulfilment of all the elect', she intercedes for its communication to men *(cf. LG 62; RM 40)*. The Blessed Virgin is therefore not just the Church's 'noblest member' *(RM 1)* and highest 'model'; (2) she is also the Church's devoted Mother, because with motherly love she co-operates in the birth and growth of the Church's sons and daughters *(RM 44)*. Holy Church is mother in and through Holy Mother Mary.

Conclusion

In *Redemptoris Mater*, Pope John Paul commends the spirituality of St Louis-Marie de Montfort, particularly his conviction that consecration to the Blessed Virgin is an effective way for Christians to live out their baptismal vows, their renunciation of Satan and their commitment, in faith, to the Blessed Trinity *(cf. RM 48)*. His words will therefore provide both a suitable summing up of the Holy Father's teaching on our Lady and the means by which we, the sons of the Church, can make that teaching our own. With the help of Louis-Marie's prayer, and guided by the mag-

isterium of John Paul, we can pledge ourselves to
belong totally to Mary and thereby totally to Jesus:

I, an unfaithful sinner, renew and ratify this day the
promises of my Baptism, and I place this renewal in
your hands, O Immaculate Mary. I renounce forever
Satan, with his works and pomps; and I give myself
entirely to Jesus Christ, the Incarnate Wisdom, that I
may carry my cross and follow Him all the days of
my life. And in order that I may be more faithful to
Him than I have hitherto been, I choose you today, O
Mary, in the presence of the whole court of Heaven,
to be my Mother and my Queen. I hand over and con-
secrate to you, as your slave, my body and my soul,
my possessions interior and exterior, even the value of
my good actions, past, present, and to come. I give
you the full and entire right to dispose of me and all
that belongs to me, without exception, in accordance
with your good pleasure, and to the greater glory of
God, both in time and eternity. Amen.

John Paul prays in front of the statue of Our Lady of Fatima, 13th May 2000.

THE NEW EVANGELIZATION

By Anthony Bosnick

Jesus Christ is at the very heart of John Paul's life and ministry. And through word and deed, John Paul has proclaimed the Good News of Jesus to the ends of the earth over the many years of his pontificate. Proclaiming the gospel is not new to John Paul as Pope. From the time he was a young priest, he took seriously his call to share the Good News among those that he served. His understanding of this call grew as he ministered to God's people as priest, bishop, and cardinal. And as pope, it is so clear to him that he sees his mission to be the "pilgrim pope of evangelization."

The Church is Missionary

When Cardinal Karol Wojtyla became Pope, he already recognized the erosion in Christian belief in the western world. From his travels as a Cardinal and from his intense interest in the world, he was no stranger to the fact that in large parts of Europe and North America the once robust Christian life was a thing of the past. His many pastoral journeys around the world have affirmed this. Over twenty years later, at the end of the Great Jubilee of 2000, he looked into the new millennium and reflected: "Even in countries evangelized many centuries ago, the reality of a 'Christian society' which ... measured itself explicitly on Gospel values is now gone" (*Novo Millennio Ineunte* 40).

This reality has not immobilized John Paul by its immensity, but rather has energized him and prompted him to call for a "new evangelization" to bring the Good News of Jesus to the world in a fresh and appealing way.

John Paul understands the Second Vatican Council (1962-65) as a time of preparation for renewed efforts of missionary activity and evangelization. He believes the teaching of the Council expressed in *Ad Gentes* (*Decree on the Church's Missionary Activity*) that "the whole Church is missionary, and the work of evangelization is a basic duty of the People of God" *(AG 35)*. In fact, in 1990, he wrote in *Redemptoris Missio* (*Mission of the Redeemer*), his major encyclical on the missionary activity of the Church, that the Council "sought to renew the Church's life and activity in the light of the needs of the contemporary world," and that one area of renewal stemming from the Council is his own emphasis on the Church's "missionary activity" around the world *(RMS 1)*.

Proclaim Christ to all Peoples

Thirteen years into his pontificate, John Paul wrote to the whole Church that after traveling "to the ends of the earth," and responding to the prompting of the Spirit to proclaim the works of God, that these travels and "direct contact with peoples who do not know Christ [have] convinced me even more of the *urgency of missionary activity* [emphasis original]" *(RMS 1)*.

Despite the many positive signs he saw, he lamented "an undeniable negative tendency" that essentially has two dimensions. First, there is a decline in missionary activity "to the nations (*ad gentes*)." This is largely to those areas of the world that were once the focus of missionary activity, such as Africa, Asia and parts of Oceania. Second, he saw the need to bring the gospel of Jesus Christ once again to those peoples who had already been evangelized and were once part of Catholic Christianity throughout the world, particularly in Europe and the Americas. He refers to this as "the new evangelization" of Christian peoples *(RMS 2)*.

John Paul called all peoples everywhere to "Open the doors to Christ." The urgency to share the Good News of Jesus is obvious in light of "the number of those who do not know Christ and do not belong to the Church," a number that has "almost doubled" since the end of the Council. About the imperative of this two-dimensional mission, John Paul wrote: "God is opening before the Church the horizons of a humanity more fully prepared for the sowing of the Gospel. I sense that the moment has come to commit all the Church's energies to a new evangelization and to the mission *ad gentes*. No believer in Christ, no institution of the Church can avoid this supreme duty: to proclaim Christ to all peoples" *(RMS 3)*.

John Paul's understanding of the call to bring the Good News to peoples everywhere is clearly two-dimensional - to the foreign missions and to people already evangelized but who have lost their belief. In the remainder of this chapter, we will focus on the "new evangelization" of those who were once Catholic Christians but who have abandoned the faith.

Pilgrim Pope of Evangelization

John Paul's efforts in evangelization and his call for the new evangelization do not occur in a vacuum. Vatican II opened the doors to a new way of thinking in the Church about evangelization. Cardinal Avery Dulles, SJ makes the point that while "evangelization" was not even mentioned in Vatican I (1869-70), it was mentioned just short of fifty times at Vatican II (Avery Dulles, "John Paul II and the New Evangelization-What Does It Mean," in *John Paul II and the New Evangelization*, 1995, p. 26). Following the Council, Pope Paul VI chose "evangelization" as the theme of the

1974 Synod of Bishops and in 1975 issued *Evangelii Nuntiandi (On Evangelization in the Modern World)*, his great exhortation on evangelization. Here Pope Paul VI called evangelization "the essential mission of the Church ... the grace and vocation proper to the church, her greatest identity." He continued, "She exists in order to evangelize" *(EN, 14)*.

Karol Wojtyla, as Archbishop of Krakow, played a significant role in the work of the Second Vatican Council, helping to draft key documents. After returning to Krakow at the end of the Council, he set to work finding ways to implement its teaching. In 1972, he published the Polish original of *Sources of Renewal* to help with the implementation of the Council's renewal agenda in his archdiocese. Evangelization through "witness-bearing" was significant in his mind, including the role of the laity in witnessing to the life of Christ in word and deed in marriage and family life and in the worlds of work, politics, and culture (Karol Wojtyla, *Sources of Renewal*, 1980, pp. 212, 217-18).

In the field of evangelization, Pope John Paul II has built on the foundations laid by Vatican II and Pope Paul VI. His thoughts and efforts had developed enough by 1990, that he could declare while on a pastoral visit in Mexico City: "The Lord and Master of history and of our destinies, has wished my pontificate to be that of a pilgrim pope of evangelization, walking down the roads of the world, bringing to all peoples the message of salvation."

The New Evangelization

On an earlier pastoral visit to Latin America in 1983, John Paul first used the expression "the new evangelization," which he characterized as "new in ardour, in methods, and in expression."

The *message* of the new evangelization is not itself new. Rather, it remains the message the Church has proclaimed throughout the ages: God sent Jesus Christ to invite us into God's life and love. Through word and deed Jesus made present God's kingdom, but was rejected by the people, suffered, died, and rose to new life. He now reigns with the Father in heaven and has sent the Holy Spirit to be with us until the end of time when he will gather all to himself for eternity. This is the same unchanging message John Paul himself has proclaimed throughout his life and pontificate.

This message is both Christ-centered and Trinitarian. John Paul writes: "The Church's universal mission is born of faith in Jesus Christ, as is stated in our Trinitarian profession of faith: 'I believe in one Lord, Jesus Christ, the only Son of God, eternally begotten of the Father... For us men and for our salvation he came down from heaven: by the power of the Holy Spirit he became incarnate from the Virgin Mary, and was made man'" *(RMS 4)*.

This message has universal and eternal significance: "Salvation can come only from Jesus Christ" *(RMS 5)*, but it comes for *all* people. "The universality of salvation means that it is granted not only to those who explicitly believe in Christ and have entered the Church. Since salvation is offered to all, it must be concretely available to all" *(RMS 10)*, a truth taught by Vatican II *(RMS 10; GS 22)*. The message must be taught in all its richness, fullness, and transforming power, for entry into this truth brings entry into the life and love of God.

New in Ardour, Methods and Expression

While the message is not new, the *way* the message is proclaimed in our own time is new. The pope is keenly aware that the Church in the modern world - and now the postmodern world - must communicate in a way that the world can understand. And thus the sensitivity in the new evangelization to the need for new ardour, methods, and expression. The content of the message has not changed, for Jesus is the same yesterday, today and forever (see *Hebrews 13:8*), but the way it is proclaimed does change, for the culture through which the message is mediated has changed - and continues to change - rapidly and radically.

Pope John Paul has not spelled out what he means by an evangelization that is new in ardour, methods and expression. He prefers, it would seem, to leave it to the local churches, organizations, ministries, and individuals to develop evangelization programs and processes that reflect the various dimensions of the new evangelization. Some of these aspects are described below.

An evangelization that is *new in ardour* reflects a renewed energy and purpose that animates efforts to share the Good News. At the heart of this new ardour is reliance on the Holy Spirit to inform, lead and guide all human efforts and programs and to generate fervor and zeal. *New methods* reflects the use of the media and electronic methods to spread the Good News, such as web sites, chat rooms and bulletin boards on the Internet, or perhaps creative use of videos and films. These new methods likely complement tried and true methods such as the spoken work in homilies, the written word in newspapers, magazines, and pamphlets, and the use of radio and television (which themselves were once new methods). *New expression* may reflect efforts to reach the postmodern world by communicating the Good News through contemporary forms of music and entertainment, or by engaging the world in discussion regarding human freedom and social advancement. The challenge of the new evangelization is to communicate the Good News to the world with energy and hope using methods that engage and language the world can comprehend.

The new evangelization differs in several ways from the evangelization efforts of the Church in previous times. Cardinal Avery Dulles has identified several of these differences.

First, the new evangelization calls for and expects the participation of every Christian, including the laity. Clearly, evangelization remains part of the missionary work of the Church, especially of the bishops, members of missionary orders both ordained and religious, and other priests and religious, and John Paul continues to encourage this work *(RMS 63-70)*. In addition, however, the laity have a central role in the new evangelization, particularly as they live out their lives in the world of family and work, and interact in the societies in which they live (*RMS 71-74*; see also *Christifideles Laici*, 34-35). He also sees the importance of the "'new movements' filled with missionary dynamism" and recommends that they "spread, and that they be used to give fresh energy ... to the Christian life and to evangelization" *(RMS 72;* see also *Message of Pope John Paul II to World Congress of Ecclesial Movements, 2).*

Second, the new evangelization is distinct from foreign missions. The Church should no longer direct its message only to traditional missionary lands in Africa, Asia, and Oceania. It now must be directed to Europe and the Americas, those lands once considered solidly Christian. In these lands, some people need primary evangelization because they have never heard the gospel while others need reevangelization to bring to life the message they have once heard but which has been trampled underfoot by the cares and concerns of the world *(RMS 33)*.

Third, the Church should direct its efforts in the new evangelization toward transformation of culture in the spirit of the gospel and seeks a comprehensive Christianization of society. John Paul believes that faith and culture are linked, and that faith serves the culture as it enlivens entertainment, the media, government and politics, and all other human interaction and activities with a spirit of truth and justice, love and hope. It uses all means available including catechesis, and the social and moral teaching of the Church. The new evangelization seeks to transform the culture of death into a civilization of life and love *(RMS 52-54)*.

Encountering Christ: A Face to Contemplate

How are we who live at the dawn of the new millennium in cultures that are often indifferent or hostile to the Good News to reflect the ardour, develop the methods, and perfect the means of expression so necessary for the new evangelization?

Pope John Paul points us to Jesus. He invites us to "contemplate his face" and to "start afresh from Christ" *(NMI 16-41)*. Just as those who lived in Jesus' day went to see him to learn more about him *(John 12:21-22)*, so the people of the world today need to meet him, contemplate his face, and learn from him. However, before today's disciples can introduce Jesus to others, we must first contemplate him ourselves. We need to make the same pilgrimage of faith made by Peter and the other apostles.

Just as Jesus asked Peter, "Who do you say that I am" *(Matthew 16:17)*, he asks the same question of us today. In addition, according to John Paul, we need to answer it with the grace of revelation that comes from the Father. We open ourselves to this grace through "the experience of silence and prayer" which allows for the "growth and development of a true, faithful and consistent knowledge of that mystery" of Christ *(NMI 20)*.

And so John Paul invites the Church to contemplate the face of Jesus in the sorrow of his suffering and death, and in the joy of his resurrection. As we gaze upon the face of Christ and contemplate the mysteries of our own lives - our joys and hopes, our griefs and sorrows - we will meet Jesus and learn of him and his love for us, just as did the saints. "Gazing on the face of Christ, the bride contemplates her treasure and joy... How sweet is the memory of Jesus, the source of the heart's true joy!" *(NMI 28, see also 25-28)*.

What does this mean in practical terms for Christians? Keeping in mind that we "are not saved by a formula" but by Jesus, John Paul exhorts the Church to seek "a genuine 'training in holiness' adapted to people's needs." At the heart of this is a "Christian life distinguished above all in the art of prayer," both personal and communal. "Prayer develops that conversation with Christ which makes us his intimate friends" *(NMI 29, 31, 32)*. This life must be nourished by the Sunday Eucharist and the "practice of the sacrament of reconciliation" *(NMI 35-37)*. In addition, to this John Paul adds the importance of listening to the word of God and courageously proclaiming it *(NMI 39, 40)*.

In these ways, we "allow ourselves to be filled with the ardour of the apostolic preaching" and we "revive in ourselves the burning conviction of Paul, who cried out, 'Woe to me if I do not preach the Gospel'." John Paul affirms his belief: "This passion will not fail to stir in the church a new sense of mission, which cannot be left to a group of 'specialists' but must involve the responsibility of all the members of the people of God. Those who have come into genuine contact with Christ cannot keep him for themselves; they must proclaim him" *(NMI 40)*.

Into the Third Millennium

At the beginning of the new millennium, John Paul expresses the burden of his heart to the Church: "The Christ whom we have contemplated and loved bids us to set out once more on our journey [to]... 'make disciples of all nations.'... The missionary mandate accompanies us into the third millennium and urges us to share the enthusiasm of the very first Christians: We count on the power of the same Spirit who was poured out at Pentecost and who impels us still today to start out anew, sustained by the hope 'which does not disappoint'" *(Romans 5:5) (NMI 58)*.

This hope sustains John Paul as he leads us in the way of the new evangelization to proclaim the Good News of Jesus to the people of our time in ways they can comprehend.

LIST OF DOCUMENTS AND ABBREVIATIONS

JOHN PAUL II'S ENCYCLICALS

Redemptor Hominis	**RH**	1979
Dives in Misericordia	**DM**	1980
Laborem Exercens	**LE**	1981
Slavorum Apostoli	**SA**	1985
Dominum et Vivificantem	**DV**	1986
Sollicitudo Rei Socialis	**SRS**	1987
Redemptoris Mater	**RM**	1987
Redemptoris Missio	**RMS**	1990
Centesimus Annus	**CA**	1991
Veritatis Splendor	**VS**	1993
Ut Unum Sint	**UUS**	1995
Evangelium Vitae	**EV**	1995
Fides et Ratio	**FR**	1998

JOHN PAUL II'S APOSTOLIC EXHORTATIONS (SELECTION)

Catechesi Tradendae	**CT**	1979
Familiaris Consortio	**FC**	1981
Christifideles Laici	**CL**	1988
Redemptoris Custos	**RC**	1989
Pastores Dabo Vobis	**PDV**	1992

JOHN PAUL II'S APOSTOLIC LETTERS (SELECTION)

Salvifici Doloris	**SD**	1984
Mulieris Dignitatem	**MD**	1988
Tertio Millennio Adveniente	**TMA**	1994
Ordinatio Sacerdotalis	**OS**	1994
Orientale Lumen	**OL**	1995
Dies Domini	**DD**	1998
Novo Millennio Ineunte	**NMI**	2001

JOHN PAUL'S LETTERS TO SPECIAL GROUPS (SELECTION)

Letter to Families	**LF**	1994
Letter to Women	**LW**	1995
Letter to the Elderly	**LE**	1999
Letter to Artists	**LA**	1999

SECOND VATICAN COUNCIL

Gaudium et Spes	**GS**	1965
Lumen Gentium	**LG**	1964
Unitatis Redintegratio	**UR**	1965